NEW HAVEN FREE PUBLIC LIBRARY
3 5000 09555 6436
P9-AQQ-836

ENGLISH LITERATURE FROM THE RESTORATION THROUGH THE ROMANTIC PERIOD

The Britannica Guide to World Literature

English Literature from the Restoration through the Romantic Period

Edited by J.E. Luebering, Manager and
Senior Editor, Literature

in association with

Published in 2011 by Britannica Educational Publishing
(a trademark of Encyclopædia Britannica, Inc.)
in association with Rosen Educational Services, LLC
29 East 21st Street, New York, NY 10010.

Distributed exclusively by Rosen Educational Services.
For a listing of additional Britannica Educational Publishing titles, call toll free (800) 237-9932.

First Edition

Britannica Educational Publishing
Michael I. Levy: Executive Editor
J.E. Luebering: Senior Manager
Marilyn L. Barton: Senior Coordinator, Production Control
Steven Bosco: Director, Editorial Technologies
Lisa S. Braucher: Senior Producer and Data Editor
Yvette Charboneau: Senior Copy Editor
Kathy Nakamura: Manager, Media Acquisition
J.E. Luebering: Senior Editor, Literature

Rosen Educational Services
Jeanne Nagle: Senior Editor
Nelson Sá: Art Director, Designer
Cindy Reiman: Photography Manager
Matthew Cauli: Designer, Cover Design
Introduction by Richard Barrington

Library of Congress Cataloging-in-Publication Data

English literature from the Restoration through the romantic period / edited by J.E. Luebering.—1st ed.
p. cm.—(The Britannica guide to world literature)
"In association with Britannica Educational Publishing, Rosen Educational Services."
Includes bibliographical references and index.
ISBN 978-1-61530-115-7 (library binding)
1. English literature—History and criticism. 2. English literature—Early modern, 1500-1700—History and criticism. 3. English literature—18th century—History and criticism. 4. English literature—19th century—History and criticism. I. Luebering, J. E.
PR83.E63 2010
820.9—dc22

2009053647 2009045098

Manufactured in the United States of America

On the cover: Influential British writers from the Restoration through the Romantic period include poet John Keats (foreground) and satirist Jonathan Swift (background). *Time & Life Pictures/Getty Images (Keats); Hulton Archive/Getty Images (Swift).*

On page 8: Frontispiece to William Blake's *Europe, A Prophecy* (1794), drawn by the author. *Peter Willi/Superstock/Getty Images*

Pages 16 (map), 226, 228, 230, 232 © www.istockphoto.com/Nicolas Belton; pp. 16 (books), 17, 51, 134 © www.istockphoto.com

CONTENTS

204
207
216
224

INTRODUCTION

By the Restoration of the English monarchy in 1660, English literature had achieved a wider popularity than ever before among all classes of English society. It had formed an identity that was distinctly English and, at its best, earned a lasting appreciation that continues to this day.

Works that had come before, by English authors such as Chaucer and Shakespeare, are clearly of a different time. There is a gulf that separates works of the Old and Middle English periods from those of the present day, and that gulf is apparent in language, style, form, and content. English literature bridged this gulf, one author at a time, largely over the period from the Restoration to the start of the Victorian era. This book examines that transformation, detailing how English literature benefited from the influences that had gone before while also developing in a manner that set the stage for the contemporary era. Readers also will delve deeply into the personalities and lives of the authors of this period who, beyond all else, brought a heightened sense of humanity to English literature.

From the Restoration to the Victorian era, many of the elements that readers associate with contemporary literature were first introduced or refined by British authors. The categories satire, political commentary, self-help, romance, horror, memoir, and journalism—all of which echo the sections found within any bookstore today—came to fruition at this time. Although they continued to struggle against disregard and disdain, women increasingly joined men in the literary marketplace, with the end of the 18th century witnessing a flourishing of women writers. Most significantly, what would become the most popular form of literature during the 19th and 20th centuries, the novel, emerged during this period.

In short, this was a period of tremendous activity and accomplishment that, oddly enough, started with a certain amount of caution. The return of the monarchy in 1660 followed 11 years of chaotic rule, first under Parliament, then under Oliver Cromwell and his son Richard. One reaction to this upheaval was the return of active censorship following the Restoration. Dissenting political views in literature, therefore, were often circulated anonymously or released posthumously. In this environment, satire became an important tool for indirectly critiquing the monarchy under Charles II and his successor, James II. One of the most active social satirists of the time, Andrew Marvell, managed to serve as a member of Parliament for 19 years while anonymously circulating works so controversial that a reward was offered for revealing the author's identity.

For some, the ultimate failure of England's experiment with republican government was a more chastening experience. John Milton, who first rose to prominence before the English Civil Wars, produced his best known work, Paradise Lost, after the Restoration. Milton had been an ardent republican, but *Paradise Lost* and his other works of this later period resonate with the poignancy of a revolution that had lost its way. Other defeated republicans limited themselves to expressing their disappointments in private memoirs, many of which were carefully edited even when being published posthumously.

While published political dissent was suppressed following the Restoration, there were numerous critiques of the established religious and social orders of the time. Those who resisted the doctrines and practices of the Church of England are known collectively as "the Nonconformists," although, appropriately, they were too diverse and unconnected to be considered part of any cohesive group or movement. Many Nonconformists produced vibrant works of literature that transcended mere theological critique. John Bunyan came to be the most noteworthy of the Nonconformists. Bunyan's masterpiece, *The Pilgrim's Progress*, broke new ground by combining theological discussion with ordinary personal experience. This achievement earned the book more readers than any other 17th-century work except for the King James Bible.

Another important characteristic of 17th-century English literature was the profusion of scientific writing, led by the works of Isaac Newton. While Newton's greatest work, *Philosophiae Naturalis Principia Mathematica*, was written in Latin for a select audience, his circle of followers grew steadily, as did Newton's influence. Inspired by Newton's writing, the philosopher John Locke brought empirical, scientific observation to the realm of philosophy, and in doing so sowed some of the earliest seeds of what was to become the modern field of psychology. In 1690, in *Two Treatises of Government*, Locke also explored the rights of people to a fair government, including the justification of rebellion when government fails to fulfill its fundamental obligations. Locke was reacting to ongoing controversies regarding the English monarchy, but his words would resonate nearly a century later during the American Revolution.

Clearly, there was an important social context to the work of Restoration writers such as Bunyan and Locke. Much is known about that context because of two observant diarists, John Evelyn and Samuel Pepys. Although not writing for public consumption, their works would provide future generations with insights into life in the second half of the 1600s, from accounts of major events such as the Great Fire and the Great Plague of London to everyday details about food and individual personalities.

Perhaps the most versatile writer of this era was John Dryden. Among other things, Dryden pioneered formal criticism of English literature, bringing to bear his own experiences as a writer, including sizable bodies of work in both poetry and drama, to help explore and explain the works of his contemporaries. He also led a surge of achievement in drama by Restoration playwrights, as perceptive comedies became the defining characteristic of this period in the theatre. Performances of Restoration plays continued to dominate the theatre well into the 18th century, and even outshone many of the dramatic works written during that century.

If 18th-century writers aren't known primarily for their dramas, perhaps it is because their attentions were elsewhere. State censorship of the press was stopped in 1695. This opened up a tremendous period for political writing, a literary form that is distinguished not just because of its historical significance, but because it attracted so many of the great writers of the day, including Daniel Defoe, Samuel Johnson, Henry Fielding, Alexander Pope, and Jonathan Swift.

Each of the aforementioned writers distinguished himself in other realms of literature as well. Johnson and Swift held reputations resting largely on their work as essayists, though they also were accomplished poets (Johnson) and novelists (Swift). As an essayist, Johnson wrote critical examinations of the human condition. As a literary critic, he helped cement Shakespeare's place as a cornerstone of English literature. Swift, meanwhile, distinguished himself with his memorable satires, including *A Modest Proposal* and *Gulliver's Travels*.

Defoe and Fielding, along with Samuel Richardson, were instrumental in the development of the novel as both a popular and artistically rich form of literature. Many early novels were epistolary in structure, which means they were written as a series of letters. While this formulation has narrative limitations, it was effective in establishing a character by revealing, by way of often intimate and immediate detail, that character's underlying attitudes, emotions, and prejudices.

It is also worth noting that as the novel rose to prominence, women authors began to make a more pronounced mark on the literary scene. Sarah Fielding (novelist Henry Fielding's sister), Charlotte Lennox, and Fanny Burney all succeeded as novelists in the 18th century. Women such as Lady Mary Montagu and Charlotte Smith also achieved publishing success as poets throughout this period, with Montagu also becoming known, posthumously, as one of the century's finest letter-writers.

The poetry produced by these and other writers of the time followed no single style or school; indeed it is noteworthy for its diversity. Conformity to rigid convention was beginning to give way to individualism and experimentation. Along with Pope, one of the most enduring poets of the 18th century is Robert Burns. Burns reinterpreted English literary traditions to express plain-spoken emotions in Scottish dialect. In keeping with the everyman quality of his writings, Burns's poems reflect a revolutionary's passion for the freedom of the individual. These sentiments captured the spirit of an age which hatched the American and French revolutions.

Although the poetry of the 18th century failed to produce any breakthroughs as significant as the emergence of the novel, it at least expanded the poetic form enough to allow for the golden era that was to follow--the age of the Romantics.

The Romantic poets may be the best-known grouping of poets in Western literary history, and yet they actually pursued a variety of different styles, and they worked over a period spanning several decades. They did not group or label themselves as "the Romantic poets," but they certainly influenced one another. Their works have several characteristics in common. Inspired by the revolutionary times that led into the Romantic period, there is a common theme of optimism that a new age was emerging, full of possibilities. More specifically, in terms of their approach to poetry, the Romantic poets represented a break from the stricter rules of their predecessors, which gave their verse a new freedom and strength of emotion.

Indeed, personal feelings are at the core of the Romantic movement. The emphasis was on conveying individual experiences, which made poetry at once more idiosyncratic and more passionate. This use of poetry to communicate a personal vision of the world is largely how poetry is still thought of to this day, but in the late 18th and early 19th centuries, the concept was quite revolutionary.

The first of these poetic revolutionaries was William Blake. Beginning with his Songs of Innocence in 1789 and continuing with *The Marriage of Heaven and Hell* and *Songs of Experience* in the early 1790s, Blake rebelled against the age of reason that he perceived around him as being too stifling. Blake sought nothing less than to create a new mythology in his attempt to find a higher meaning to existence than the logical explanations of science.

Blake was followed by Samuel Taylor Coleridge and William Wordsworth, whose work continued into the 19th century. Coleridge and Wordsworth often turned to observations of nature to explore the human condition, with Coleridge taking a mystical approach in poems such as *The Rime of the Ancient Mariner and Kubla Khan*.

Coleridge and Wordsworth both had an affect on a slightly younger generation of poets, including Percy

Bysshe Shelley, John Keats, and George Gordon Byron (better known as Lord Byron). The fact that all these extraordinary poets were at the height of their powers in the first quarter of the 19th century explains why the Romantic period stands so prominently in the history of poetry.

The later Romantic period also saw the novel become even more fully realized, after having gone through a somewhat fallow period for nearly half a century following the highly productive years of the mid-1700s. Perhaps the most noteworthy development in late 18th-century prose fiction was the creation of the Gothic novel, which combined elements of horror with strong undercurrents of (sometimes deviant) psychology and sexuality. This form, which remains popular to this day, has some useful applications for social commentary, though it also has a tendency toward melodrama and exploitation.

In the second decade of the 1800s, the landscape for novels changed yet again with the publication of works by Jane Austen and Sir Walter Scott. Austen's incisive wit and Scott's sense of grandeur each helped bring the novel to new heights.

As this volume illustrates, the period from the Restoration through the Romantic era introduced many of the elements considered essential to English literature today. Poetry found a new freedom, and the novel emerged as a dominant form. Overall, writing became more personal and achieve a new sense of humanity, and that's perhaps the most modern characteristic to emerge from this period.

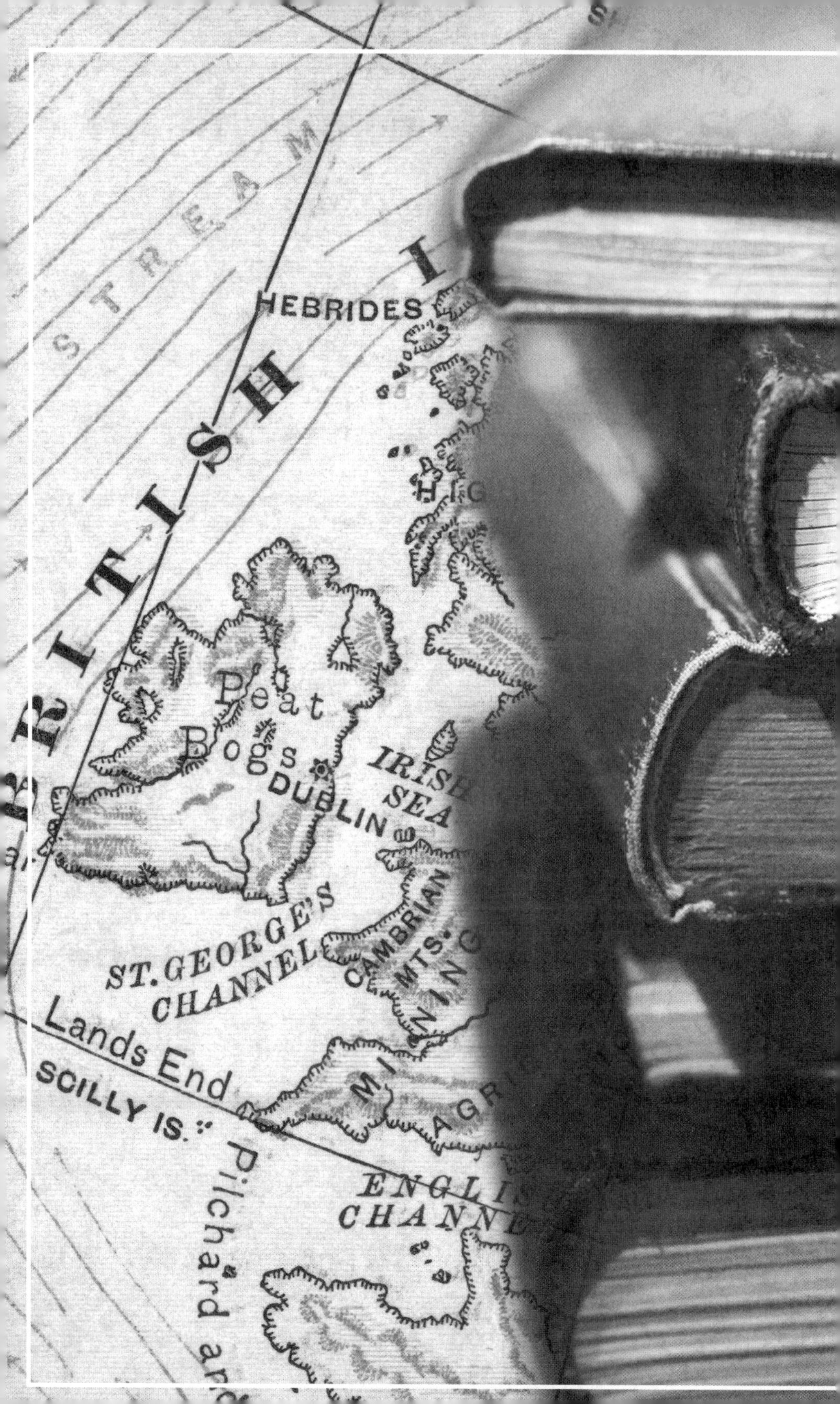
STREAM
HEBRIDES
Peat Bogs
DUBLIN
ST. GEORGE'S CHANNEL
CAMBRIAN MTS.
Lands End
SCILLY IS.

RESTORATION LITERATURE

The term *Restoration literature* refers to literature written after the Restoration of the English monarchy in 1660. Many of the literary forms considered typical of the modern world—including the novel, biography, history, travel writing, and journalism—were either invented or reached maturity in the late 17th century. Writers in all of these forms gained confidence, and wider readerships, during the Restoration period, when new scientific discoveries and philosophical concepts, as well as new social and economic conditions, came into play. There was a great outpouring of pamphlet literature, too, much of it politico-religious, while John Bunyan's great allegory, *Pilgrim's Progress,* also belongs to this period. Much of the best poetry, notably that of John Dryden (the great literary figure of his time, in both poetry and prose), was satirical and led directly to the later achievements of Alexander Pope, Jonathan Swift, and John Gay in the 18th century. The Restoration period was, above all, a great age of drama. Heroic plays, influenced by principles of French Neoclassicism, enjoyed a vogue, but the age is chiefly remembered for its glittering, critical comedies of manners by such playwrights as George Etherege, William Wycherley, Sir John Vanbrugh, and William Congreve.

For some, the restoration of King Charles II in 1660 led to a painful revaluation of the political hopes and millenarian expectations bred during two decades that witnessed the violence and disorder of the English Civil Wars (1642–51) and the subsequent emergence of republican government under Oliver Cromwell. For others, it excited the desire to celebrate kingship and even to turn the events of the new reign into signs of a divinely ordained scheme of things. Violent political conflict may have ceased, but the division between royalists and republicans still ran through literature of the period. Indeed, it is hard to conceive of a single literary culture that could include, on the one hand, Bunyan and John Milton and, on the other, Dryden and John Wilmot, earl of Rochester. Yet these and other such opposites were writing at the same time.

Some literary historians speak of the period as bounded solely by the reign of Charles II (1660–85), but the term as used here also includes works produced during the reign of James II (1685–88) as well as some literature of the 1690s. By the last decade of the 17th century, however, the reign of William III and Mary II (1689–1702) had begun, and the ethos of courtly and urban fashion had become sober, Protestant, and even pious, in contrast to the sexually and intellectually libertine spirit of court life under Charles II.

Restoration literature is often taken to mean the literature of those who belonged, or aspired to belong, to the restored court culture of Charles II's reign—the "mob of gentlemen who wrote with ease," as Pope later put it. This identification was to allow Pope's contemporaries to look back on the Restoration as an age of excess and licentiousness. Yet Puritans and republicans had not disappeared. With the Act of Uniformity (1662) and the Test Act (1673), those Protestants not conforming with the Church of England ("Dissenters") were excluded from most public offices. However, they still formed an important body of opinion within the nation. They were also to make a

A sitting member of Parliament during the Restoration, Andrew Marvell was a master of political satire. The handful of Marvell's works published in his lifetime were done so anonymously. Archive Photos/Getty Images

distinctive contribution to the nation's intellectual life throughout the following century.

In the first years after Charles II's return, dissent was stilled or secretive. With the return of an efficient censorship, ambitiously heterodox ideas in theology and politics that had found their way freely into print during the 1640s and 1650s were once again denied publication. For erstwhile supporters of Cromwell's Commonwealth, the experience of defeat needed time to be absorbed, and fresh strategies had to be devised to encounter the challenge of hostile times. Much caustic and libelous political satire was written during the reigns of Charles II and James II that, because printing was subject to repressive legal constrictions, was circulated anonymously, widely in manuscript.

Andrew Marvell, sitting as member of Parliament for Hull in three successive Parliaments from 1659 to 1678, experimented energetically with this mode. His *Last Instructions to a Painter* (written in 1667) achieves a control of a broad canvas and an alertness to apt detail and the movement of the masses that make it a significant forerunner of Pope's *Dunciad*, however divergent the two poets' political visions may be. Marvell also proved himself to be a dexterous, abrasive prose controversialist, comprehensively deriding the anti-Dissenter arguments of Samuel Parker (later bishop of Oxford) in *The Rehearsal Transprosed* (1672, with a sequel in 1673) and providing so vivid an exposition of Whig suspicions of the restored monarchy's attraction to absolutism in *An Account of the Growth of Popery and Arbitrary Government in England* (1677) that a reward of £100 was offered for revealing its author's identity.

THE DEFEATED REPUBLICANS

The greatest prose controversialist of the pre-1660 years, John Milton, did not return to that mode but, in his enforced retirement from the public scene, devoted himself to his great poems of religious struggle and conviction, *Paradise Lost* (1667, revised 1674) and *Paradise Regained* and

Samson Agonistes (both 1671). Each, in its probing of the intricate ways in which God's design reveals itself in human history, can justly be read (in one of its dimensions) as a chastened but resolute response to the failure of a revolution in which Milton himself had placed great trust and hope.

Others of the defeated republicans set out to record their own or others' experiences in the service of what they called the "good old cause." Lucy Hutchinson composed, probably in the mid-1660s, her remarkable memoirs of the life of her husband, Colonel John Hutchinson, the parliamentarian commander of Nottingham during the Civil Wars. Edmund Ludlow, like Hutchinson one of the regicides, fled to Switzerland in 1660, where he compiled his own *Memoirs*. These were published only in 1698–99, after Ludlow's death, and the discovery in 1970 of part of Ludlow's own manuscript revealed that they had been edited and rewritten by another hand before printing.

Civil War testimony still had political applications in the last years of the 17th century, but those who sponsored its publication judged that Ludlow's now old-fashioned, millenarian rhetoric should be suppressed in favour of a soberer commonwealthman's dialect. Some autobiographers adjusted their testimony themselves in the light of later developments. The Quaker leader George Fox, for example, dictating his *Journal* to various amanuenses, dubiously claimed for himself an attachment to pacifist principles during the 1650s, whereas it was in fact only in 1661, in the aftermath of the revolution's defeat, that the peace principle became central to Quakerism. The *Journal* itself reached print in 1694 (again, after its author's death) only after revision by a group superintended by William Penn. Such caution suggests a lively awareness of the influence such a text could have in consolidating a sect's sense of its own identity and continuity.

WRITINGS OF THE NONCONFORMISTS

John Bunyan's *Grace Abounding* (1666), written while he was imprisoned in Bedford jail for nonconformity with the Church of England, similarly relates the process of his own conversion for the encouragement of his local, dissenter congregation. It testifies graphically to the force, both terrifying and consolatory, with which the biblical word could work upon the consciousness of a scantily educated, but overwhelmingly responsive, 17th-century believer. The form of *Grace Abounding* has numerous precedents in spiritual autobiography of the period, but with *The Pilgrim's Progress* (the first part of which appeared in 1678) Bunyan found himself drawn into a much more novel experiment, developing an ambitious allegorical narrative when his intent had been to write a more conventionally ordered account of the processes of redemption. The resulting work (with its second part appearing in 1684) combines a careful exposition of the logical structure of the Calvinist scheme of salvation with a delicate responsiveness to the ways in which his experience of his own world (of the life of the road, of the arrogance of the rich, of the rhythms of contemporary speech) can be deployed to render with a new vividness the strenuous testing the Christian soul must undergo.

Bunyan's achievement owes scarcely anything to the literary culture of his time, but his masterpiece has gained for itself a readership greater than that achieved by any other English 17th-century work with the exception of the King James Bible. In the 17th and 18th centuries there were chapbook versions, at two or three pence each, for the barely literate, and there were elegant editions for pious gentlefolk. It was the favourite work of both the

Portrait of John Bunyan, a preacher whose nonconformist bent landed him in jail for crimes against the Church of England. Out of this experience sprang Grace Abounding, *his spiritual autobiography*. Hulton Archive/Getty Images

self-improving artisan and the affluent tradesman. Yet it was below the horizon of polite literary taste.

Perhaps Bunyan, born in 1628 and the uneducated son of a tinker, would have found such condescension appropriate. His writing crackles with suspicion of "gentlemen" and those who have learned eloquence, such as the impressive Mr. Worldly-Wiseman, who almost persuades Christian to self-destruction in *Pilgrim's Progress*. This work

Intended as a straightforward treatise on salvation, Bunyan's Pilgrim's Progress *is the allegorical tale of young Christian (pictured here in a 19th-century illustration) as he travels the road to redemption.* Hulton Archive/Getty Images

is also rich in disdainful portraits of those who are more than satisfied with the ways of the world: the "honourable friends" of Prince Beelzebub, such as "the Lord Luxurious, the Lord Desire of Vain-glory, my old Lord Lechery, Sir Having Greedy, with all the rest of our nobility." Bunyan had an ear for the self-satisfied conversational turns of those convinced by their own affluence that

"God has bestowed upon us the good things of this life." Two other works of his, though lesser in stature, are especially worth reading: *The Life and Death of Mr. Badman* (1680), which, with graphic local detail, remorselessly tracks the sinful temptations of everyday life, and *The Holy War* (1682), a grandiose attempt at religious mythmaking interlaced with contemporary political allusions.

Richard Baxter, a Nonconformist cleric who, although enduring persecution after 1660, was by instinct and much of his practice a reconciler, published untiringly on religious issues. Soon after the death of his wife, he wrote the moving *Breviate* (1681), a striking combination of exemplary narrative and unaffectedly direct reporting of the nature of their domestic life. His finest work, however, is the *Reliquiae Baxterianae* (published in 1696, five years after his death), an autobiography that is also an eloquent defense of the Puritan impulse in the 17th-century Christian tradition.

In the aftermath of the Restoration, there was much formulaic satirizing of Puritans, especially on the stage. A more engaging voice of anti-Puritan reaction can be heard in Samuel Butler's extensive mock-heroic satire *Hudibras* (published in three installments between 1662 and 1678). This was a massively popular work, with an influence stretching well into the 18th century (when Samuel Johnson, for example, greatly admired it and William Hogarth illustrated some scenes from it). It reads partly as a consummately destructive act of revenge upon those who had usurped power in the previous two decades, but although it is easy to identify what *Hudibras* opposes, it is difficult to say what, if anything, it affirms. Although much admired by royalist opinion, it shows no wish to celebrate the authority or person restored in 1660, and its brazenly undignified use of rhyming tetrameters mirrors, mocks, and lacerates rooted human follies far beyond the power of one political reversal to obliterate. A comparable sardonic disenchantment is apparent in Butler's shorter verse satires and in his incisive and densely argued collection of prose *Characters.*

WRITINGS OF THE ROYALISTS

Royalists also resorted to biography and autobiography to record their experiences of defeat and restoration. Three of the most intriguing are by women: the life written by Margaret, duchess of Newcastle, of her husband (1667) and the memoirs of Ann, Lady Fanshawe, and of Anne, Lady Halkett. The latter two were both written in the late 1670s but as private texts, with no apparent thought of publication. (They were not published in any complete form until, respectively, 1829 and 1875.) But incomparably the richest account of those years is *The History of the Rebellion and Civil Wars in England* by Edward Hyde, earl of Clarendon. The work was begun in exile during the late 1640s and was revised and completed in renewed exile after Clarendon's fall from royal favour in 1667. Clarendon was a close adviser to two kings, and his intimacy with many of the key events is unrivaled. Though his narrative is inevitably partisan, the ambitious range of his analysis and his mastery of character portraiture make the *History* an extraordinary accomplishment. His autobiography, which he also wrote during his last exile, gravely chronicles the transformations of the gentry world between the 1630s and 1660s.

In 1660, feeling in the country ran strongly in favour of the Church of England, persecution having confirmed in many a deep affection for Anglican rites and ceremonies. The reestablished church, accepting for itself the role of staunch defender of kingly authority, tended to eschew the exploration of ambitious and controversial theological issues and devoted itself instead to expounding codes of sound moral conduct. It was an age of eminent preachers—including Robert South, Isaac Barrow, Edward Stillingfleet, and John Tillotson—and of keen interest in the art of preaching. It was also an age in which representatives of the established church were often suspicious of the power of preaching, fearing its power to arouse "enthusiasm." This was the power that had helped excite the sectarians who had rebelled against their king. It was the power wielded by men such as Bunyan, who was imprisoned for preaching without a license.

In conscious reaction against the obscurantist dialects judged typical of the sects, a plain and direct style of sermon oratory was favoured. Thus, in his funeral sermon on Tillotson in 1694, Gilbert Burnet praised the archbishop because he "said what was just necessary to give clear Ideas of things, and no more" and "laid aside all long and affected Periods." Sermons continued to be published and to sell in large numbers throughout the late 17th and the 18th centuries.

MAJOR GENRES AND AUTHORS OF THE PERIOD

A comparable preference for an unembellished and perspicuous use of language is apparent in much of the nontheological literature of the age. Thomas Sprat, in his propagandizing *History of the Royal Society of London* (1667), and with the needs of scientific discovery in mind, also advocated "a close, naked natural way of speaking, positive expressions, clear senses, a native easiness." Sprat's work and a series of books by Joseph Glanvill, beginning with *The Vanity of Dogmatizing* (1661), argued the case for an experimental approach to natural phenomena against both the old scholastic philosophy and general conservative prejudice. That a real struggle was involved can be seen from the invariably disparaging attitude of contemporary satires to the labours of the Royal Society's enthusiasts (see, for instance, Butler's *The Elephant in the Moon*, probably written in 1670–71, and Thomas Shadwell's *The Virtuoso*, 1676)—a tradition to be sustained later by Pope and Jonathan Swift.

However, evidence of substantial achievement for the new generation of explorers was being published throughout the period, in, for example, Robert Boyle's *Sceptical Chymist* (1661), Robert Hooke's *Micrographia* (1665), John Ray's *Historia Plantarum* (in three volumes, 1686–1704), and, above all, Isaac Newton's *Philosophiae Naturalis Principia Mathematica* (1687). Newton's great work, composed in Latin, was written for fellow mathematicians rather than for gentlemen virtuosi. Only a select few were able to follow his workings (though his later *Opticks* [1704] was aimed at a much wider readership). Yet his theories were popularized by a small regiment of Newtonians, and by the early 18th century he had become a hero of his culture.

The greatest philosopher of the period, John Locke, explicitly acknowledges Newton and some of his fellow "natural philosophers" in the opening of his *An Essay Concerning Human Understanding* (1690). Locke declared himself to be an "underlabourer" to what today is called a "scientist." The philosopher's role, according to Locke, was to clear up misunderstandings, purge language of its mystifications, and call us to acknowledge the modesty of what we can know. The *Essay* was a founding text of empiricism, arguing that all knowledge comes from experience, rationally reflected upon. Empiricism rejects a belief in innate ideas and argues that the mind at birth is a tabula rasa. Experience of the world can be accumulated only through the senses, which are themselves prone to unreliability. The *Essay*, cautiously concerned to define the exact limits of what the mind can truly claim to know, threw exciting new light on the workings of human intelligence and stimulated further debate and exploration through the fertility of its suggestions—for example, about the way in which ideas come to be associated. It was hugely influential throughout the 18th century.

Locke was also a pioneer in political thought. He came from Puritan stock and was closely linked during the Restoration with leading Whig figures, especially the most controversial of them all, Anthony Ashley Cooper, 1st earl of Shaftesbury. Locke's *Two Treatises of Government*, published in 1690 but written mainly during the Exclusion Crisis—the attempt to exclude Charles II's brother James, a Roman Catholic, from succeeding to the throne—10 years earlier, asserts the right of resistance to unjust authority and, in the last resort, of revolution. To make this argument, he had to think radically about the origins of civil society, the mutual obligations of subjects and rulers, and the rights of property. The resulting work became the crucial reference point from which subsequent debate took its bearings.

Chroniclers

The Restoration, in its turn, bred its own chroniclers. *Anthony à Wood*, the Oxford antiquarian, made in his Athenae Oxonienses (1691–92) the first serious attempt at an English biographical dictionary. His labours were aided by John Aubrey, whose own unsystematic but enticing manuscript notes on the famous have been published in modern times under the title *Brief Lives*. After 1688, secret histories of the reigns of Charles II and James II were popular, of which the outstanding instance, gossipy but often reliable, is the *Memoirs of the Count Grammont*, compiled in French by Anthony Hamilton and first translated into English in 1714. A soberer but still free-speaking two-volume *History of My Own Time* (published posthumously, 1724–34) was composed by the industrious Gilbert Burnet, bishop of Salisbury from 1689. In the last months of the life of the court poet John Wilmot, 2nd earl of Rochester, Burnet had been invited to attend him, and, in *Some Passages of the Life and Death of John, Earl of Rochester* (1680), he offered a fascinating account of their conversations as the erstwhile rake edged toward a rapprochement with the faith he had spurned. Burnet's account of Rochester's final faith and penitence has been doubted by many, yet some of the dialogues that he records seem too unorthodox to be inventions.

A sparer, more finely focused prose was written by George Savile, 1st marquess of Halifax, who, closely involved in the political fray for 35 years but remaining distrustful of any simple party alignments, wrote toward the end of his life a series of thoughtful, wryly observant essays, including *The Character of a Trimmer* (circulated in manuscript in late 1684 or very early 1685), *A Letter to a Dissenter* (published clandestinely in 1687), and *A Character of King Charles the Second* (written after about 1688). He also composed for his own daughter *The Lady's New-Year's-Gift; or, Advice to a Daughter* (1688), in which he anatomizes, with a sombre but affectionate wit, the pitfalls awaiting a young gentlewoman in life, especially in marriage.

Diarists

Two great diarists, John Evelyn and Samuel Pepys, are among the most significant witnesses to the development of the Restoration world. Both possessed formidably active and inquisitive intelligences.

Evelyn was a man of some moral rectitude and therefore often unenamoured of the conduct he observed in court circles. But his curiosity was insatiable, whether the topic in question happened to be Tudor architecture, contemporary horticulture, or the details of sermon rhetoric.

Born in 1620, Evelyn wrote some 30 books on the fine arts, forestry, and religious topics. His *Diary,* kept all his life, is considered an invaluable source of information on the social, cultural, religious, and political life of 17th-century England. After studying in the Middle Temple, London, and at Balliol College, Oxford, Evelyn, the son of a wealthy landowner, decided not to join the Royalist cause in the English Civil War for fear of endangering his brother's estate at Wotton, then in parliamentary territory. In 1643, therefore, he went abroad, first to France and then to Rome, Venice, and Padua, returning to Paris in 1646. The following year he married Mary, daughter of Sir Richard Browne, Charles I's diplomatic representative to France. In 1652, during the Commonwealth, he returned to England and acquired his father-in-law's estate, Sayes Court, at Deptford. In 1659 he published two Royalist pamphlets.

At the Restoration of the monarchy in 1660, Evelyn was well received by Charles II. He served on a variety of commissions, including those concerned with London street improvement (1662), the Royal Mint (1663), and the repair of old St. Paul's (1666). Far more important was the commission for sick and wounded mariners and prisoners of war in Charles II's Dutch Wars (1665–67, 1672–74), during which Evelyn exposed himself to plague and incurred personal expenses, reimbursement for which he was still petitioning in 1702. At that time he received help from Samuel Pepys (then a navy official), with whom he formed a lifelong friendship.

Evelyn served on a council for colonial affairs from 1671 to 1674. He was appointed to the council of the Royal Society by its first and second charters in 1662 and 1663 and remained a lifelong member. In this capacity in 1664 he produced for the commissioners of the navy *Sylva, or a Discourse of Forest-trees, and the Propagation of Timber,* a description of the various kinds of trees, their cultivation, and uses. The study, with numerous modifications, had gone through 10 editions by 1825. In 1662 Evelyn produced *Sculptura,* a small book on engraving and etching, in which he announced a new process, the mezzotint.

About 1670 Evelyn formed a paternal affection for Margaret Blagge, a maid of honour at court, who later secretly married Sidney Godolphin, future lord high treasurer. She died after giving birth to a child in 1678. Evelyn's *Life of Mrs. Godolphin*, first published in 1847, is one of the most moving of 17th-century biographies.

In 1685, a few months after James II's accession, Evelyn was appointed one of three commissioners for the privy seal, an office he held for 15 months. Evelyn's last important book, *Numismata,* was published in 1697. He died nine years later.

Evelyn's *Diary,* begun when he was 11 years old and first published in 1818, was written for himself alone but with relatively little about himself in it. It ranges from bald memoranda to elaborate set pieces. With its descriptions of places and events, characters of contemporaries, and many reports of sermons, it bears witness to more than 50 years of English life and, as such, is of great historical value.

Samuel Pepys, whose diary, unlike Evelyn's, covers only the first decade of the Restoration, was the more self-scrutinizing of the two, constantly mapping his own behaviour with an alert and quizzical eye. He also described major public events from close up, including the Great Plague and the Great Fire of London and a naval war against the Dutch. Though not without his own moral inhibitions and religious gravity, Pepys immersed himself more totally than Evelyn in the new world of the 1660s, and it is he who gives the more resonant and idiosyncratic images of the changing London of the time.

Pepys's Life

Born in 1633, Pepys (pronounced *peeps*) was the son of a working tailor who had moved to London from Huntingdonshire, in which county, and in Cambridgeshire, his family had lived for centuries as monastic reeves, rent collectors, farmers, and, more recently, small gentry. His mother, Margaret Kite, was the sister of a Whitechapel butcher. But, though of humble parentage, Pepys rose to be one of the most important men of his day, becoming England's earliest secretary of the Admiralty and serving in his time as member of Parliament, president of the Royal Society (in which office he placed his imprimatur on the title page of England's greatest scientific work, Sir Isaac Newton's *Philosophiae Naturalis Principia Mathematica*), master of Trinity House and of the Clothworkers' Company, and a baron of the Cinque Ports. He was the trusted confidant both of Charles II, from whom he took down in shorthand the account of his escape after the Battle of Worcester, and of James II, whose will he witnessed before the royal flight in 1688. The friends of his old age included Sir Christopher Wren, Sir Isaac Newton, John Evelyn, Sir Godfrey Kneller, John Dryden, and almost every great scholar of the age.

Pepys was sent, after early schooling at Huntingdon, to St. Paul's School, London. In 1650 he was entered at Trinity Hall, Cambridge, but instead went as a sizar to Magdalene College, obtaining a scholarship on the foundation. In March 1653 he took his B.A. degree and in 1660 that of M.A. Little is known of his university career save that he was once admonished for being "scandalously overserved

Samuel Pepys's account of his experiences in politics as a naval administrator, combined with a colourful personal life in London, is one of the most enduring diaries in the English language. Hulton Archive/Getty Images

with drink." In later years he became a great benefactor of his college, to which he left his famous library of books and manuscripts. He was also once offered—but refused—the provostship of King's College, Cambridge.

In December 1655 he married a penniless beauty of 15, Elizabeth Marchant de Saint-Michel, daughter of a French Huguenot refugee. At this time he was employed as factotum in the Whitehall lodgings of his cousin Adm. Edward Montagu, later 1st earl of Sandwich, who was high in the lord protector Cromwell's favour. In his diary Pepys recalls this humble beginning, when his young wife "used to make coal fires and wash my foul clothes with her own hand for me, poor wretch! in our little room at Lord Sandwich's; for which I ought forever to love and admire her, and do." While there, on March 26, 1658, he underwent a serious abdominal operation, thereafter always celebrating the anniversary of his escape by a dinner—"This being my solemn feast for my cutting of the stone."

Career

In 1659 Pepys accompanied Montagu on a voyage to the Sound. About the same time he was appointed to a clerkship of £50 per annum in the office of George Downing, one of the tellers of the Exchequer, after whom Downing Street was later named. It was while working in Downing's office and living in a small house in Axe Yard that on Jan. 1, 1660, he began his diary. A few months later he sailed, as his cousin's secretary, with the fleet that brought back Charles II from exile. Appointed, through Montagu's interest at court, clerk of the acts of the navy at a salary of £350 per annum and given an official residence in the navy office in Seething Lane, he became in the next few years a justice of the peace, a commissioner for and, later, treasurer of, Tangier, and surveyor of naval victualling.

When he entered upon his functions, he was ignorant of almost everything that belonged to them. His chief use of his position was to enjoy his newfound importance and the convivial companionship of his colleagues, admirals Sir William Batten and Sir William Penn. But early in 1662 there came a change. The colleagues whose bacchanalian habits and social position had made them so attractive began to prove irksome, and their insistence on their superior experience and status galled Pepys's pride. In his isolation, he sought for ways by which he could show himself their equal. He had not far to look, for his fellow officers were anything but attentive to business. "So to the office," Pepys wrote, "where I do begin to be exact in my duty there and exacting my privileges and shall continue to do so." He had found his vocation.

It was not in Pepys's nature to do things by halves. Having resolved to do his duty, he set out to equip himself for its performance. In the summer of 1662 he occupied his leisure moments by learning the multiplication table, listening to lectures on shipbuilding, and studying the prices of naval stores: ". . . into Thames Street, beyond the Bridge, and there enquired among the shops the price of tar and oil, and do find great content in it, and hope to save the King money by this practise." At the same time, he began his habit of making careful entries of all contracts and memoranda in large vellum books—beautifully ruled by Elizabeth Pepys and her maids—and of keeping copies of his official letters.

The qualities of industry and devotion to duty that Pepys brought to the service of the Royal Navy became realized during the Second Dutch War of 1665–67—years in which he remained at his post throughout the Plague and saved the navy office in the Great Fire of London. Before trouble with his eyesight caused him to discontinue his diary in 1669—an event followed by the death of his wife—these qualities had won him the trust of the king and his brother James, the duke of York, the lord high admiral. In 1673, in the middle of the Third Dutch War, when York's unpopular conversion to Catholicism forced him to resign his office, Pepys was appointed secretary to the new commission of Admiralty and, as such, administrative head of the navy. In order to represent it in Parliament—before whom he had conducted a masterly defense of his office some years before—he became member first for Castle Rising and, later, for Harwich. For the next six years he was engaged in stamping out the corruption that had paralyzed the activities of the navy. His greatest achievement was carrying through Parliament a program that, by laying down 30 new ships of the line, restored the balance of sea power, upset by the gigantic building programs of France and the Netherlands.

In his work both at the Admiralty and in Parliament, Pepys's unbending passion for efficiency and honesty (combined with a certain childlike insistence on his own virtue and capacity for being always in the right) made for him powerful and bitter enemies. One of these was Lord Shaftesbury, who in 1678 endeavoured to strike at the succession and at the Catholic successor, the Duke of York, by implicating Pepys in the mysterious murder of the London magistrate Sir Edmund Berry Godfrey, the crime on which the full credulity of the populace in the Popish Plot depended. When Pepys produced an unanswerable alibi, his enemies endeavoured to fasten Godfrey's murder on him indirectly by accusing his confidential clerk, Samuel Atkins. Despite the third-degree methods employed against him, Pepys also proved an alibi for Atkins, who would otherwise almost certainly have perished.

Six months later, his enemies brought into England a picturesque scoundrel and blackmailer called John Scott, who had begun his life of crime in what today is Long Island, New York, and whom Pepys had endeavoured to have arrested at the time of Godfrey's death on account of his mysterious activities disguised as a Jesuit. Pepys was flung into the Tower on an absurd charge of treason brought against him by Scott and supported by the Exclusionists in Parliament, as also on a minor and equally unjust charge of popery, brought against him by a dismissed butler whom he had caught in bed with his favourite maid. Had not Charles II almost immediately dissolved Parliament and prevented a new one from meeting for a further year and a half, Pepys would have paid the penalty for his loyalty, efficiency, and incorruptibility with his life. He employed his respite with such energy that by the time Parliament met again he had completely blasted the reputation of his accuser.

In 1683, when the king felt strong enough to ignore his opponents, Pepys was taken back into the public service. He had accompanied the Duke of York in the previous year on a voyage to Scotland, and he now sailed as adviser to the Earl of Dartmouth to evacuate the English garrison of Tangier—a voyage that he described in a further journal.

On his return, in the spring of 1684, he was recalled by Charles II to his old post. Entitled secretary of the affairs of the Admiralty of England and remunerated by a salary of £500 per annum, he combined the modern offices of first lord and secretary of the Admiralty, both administering the service and answering for it in Parliament. For the next four and a half years, including the whole of James II's reign, Pepys was one of the greatest men in England, controlling the largest spending department of state. With his habitual courage and industry, he set himself to rebuild the naval edifice that the inefficiency and corruption of his enemies had shattered, securing in 1686 the appointment of a special commission "for the Recovery of the Navy." When, at the beginning of 1689, after James II had been driven from the country, Pepys retired, he had created a navy strong enough to maintain a long ascendancy in the world's seas. When Pepys became associated with the navy in 1660, the line of battle had consisted of 30 battleships of a total burden of approximately 25,000 tons and carrying 1,730 guns. When he laid down his office, he left a battle line of 59 ships of a total burden of 66,000 tons and carrying 4,492 guns. Not only had he doubled the navy's fighting strength, but he had given it what it had never possessed before and what it never again lost—a great administrative tradition of order, discipline, and service.

"To your praises," declared the orator of Oxford University, "the whole ocean bears witness; truly, sir, you have encompassed Britain with wooden walls." Pepys's last 14 years, despite attempts by his political adversaries to molest him, were spent in honourable retirement in his riverside house in York Buildings, amassing and arranging the library that he ultimately left to Magdalene College, Cambridge, corresponding with scholars and artists, and collecting material for a history of the navy that he never lived to complete, though he published a prelude to it in 1690, describing his recent work at the Admiralty, entitled *Memoires relating to the State of the Royal Navy of England for ten years determined December 1688*.

In 1703 he died at the Clapham home of his former servant and lifelong friend William Hewer. Evelyn wrote of him: "He was universally belov'd, hospitable, generous, learned in many things, skilled in music, a very greate cherisher of learned men of whom he had the conversation."

The Diary

The diary by which Pepys is chiefly known was kept between his 27th and 36th years. Written in Thomas Shelton's system of shorthand, or tachygraphy, with the names in longhand, it extends to 1,250,000 words, filling six quarto volumes in the Pepys Library. It is far more than an ordinary record of its writer's thoughts and actions; it is a supreme work of art, revealing on every page the capacity for selecting the small, as well as the large, essential that

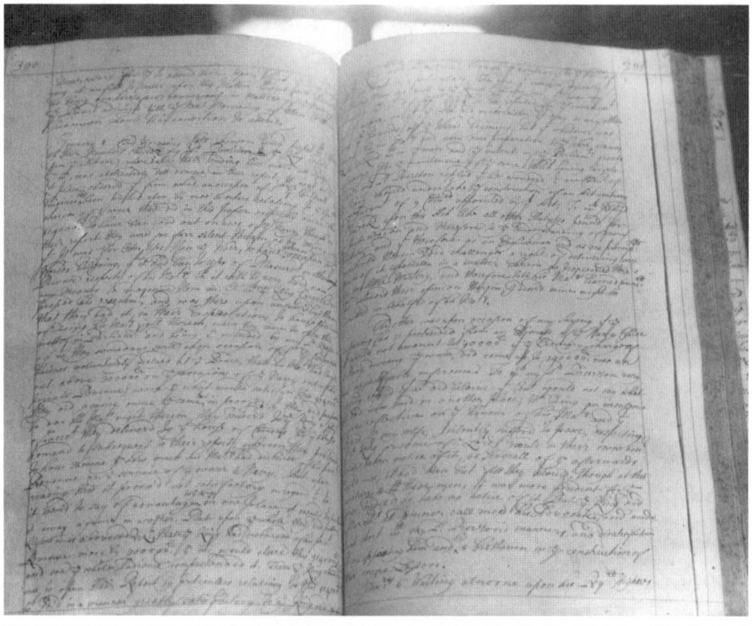

One of the volumes of Samuel Pepys's diary, housed in the library that bears the author's name at Magdalene College, Cambridge. More than 1.25 million words fill the diary's six volumes. H. Todd/Hulton Archive/Getty Images

conveys the sense of life. One can open it on any page and lose oneself in the life of Charles II's London, and of this vigorous, curious, hardworking, pleasure-loving man.

Pepys wanted to find out about everything because he found everything interesting. He never seemed to have a dull moment; he could not, indeed, understand dullness. One of the more comical entries in his diary refers to a country cousin, named Stankes, who came to stay with him in London. Pepys had been looking forward to showing him the sights of the town:

> *But Lord! what a stir Stankes makes, with his being crowded in the streets, and wearied in walking in London, and would not be wooed by my wife and Ashwell to go to a play, nor to White Hall, or to see the lions, though he was carried in a*

coach. I never could have thought there had been upon earth a man so little curious in the world as he is.

Pepys possessed the journalist's gift of summing up a scene or person in a few brilliant, arresting words. He makes us see what he sees in a flash: his Aunt James, "a poor, religious, well-meaning, good soul, talking of nothing but God Almighty, and that with so much innocence that mightily pleased me"; and his sister Pall, "a pretty, good-bodied woman and not over thick, as I thought she would have been, but full of freckles and not handsome in the face." He could describe with wonderful vividness a great scene. For example, the day General George Monck's soldiers unexpectedly marched into a sullen City and proclaimed there should be a free Parliament, he wrote, "And Bow bells and all the bells in all the churches as we went home were a-ringing; it was past imagination, both the greatness and suddenness of it." He described, too, the Restoration and coronation, the horrors of the Plague, and the Fire of London, writing down his account of the last—so strong was the artist in him—even as his home and its treasures were being threatened with destruction:

We saw the fire as only one entire arch of fire from this to the other side of the bridge, and in a bow up the hill for an arch of above a mile long: it made me weep to see it. The churches, houses, and all on fire and flaming at once; and a horrid noise the flames made, and the cracking of houses at their ruine.

Above all, Pepys possessed the artist's gift of being able to select the vital moment. He makes his readers share the very life of his time: "I staid up till the bell-man came by with his bell just under my window as I was writing of this very line, and cried, 'Past one of the clock, and a cold, and frosty, windy morning.'" He tells of the guttering candle, "which makes me write thus slobberingly"; of his new watch, "But Lord! to see how much of my old folly and childishness hangs on me still that I cannot forebear carrying my watch in my hand in the coach all the afternoon and seeing what o'clock it is one hundred times"; of being awakened in the night:

> *About 3 o'clock this morning I waked with the noise of the rain, having never in my life heard a more violent shower; and then the cat was locked in the chamber and kept a great mewing and leapt upon the bed, which made me I could not sleep a great while.*

Pepys excluded nothing from his journal that seemed to him essential, however much it told against himself. He not only recorded his major infidelities and weaknesses; he put down all those little meannesses of thought and conduct of which all men are guilty but few admit, even to themselves. He is frank about his vanity. For example, in his account of the day he went to church for the first time in his new periwig, he wrote, "I found that my coming in a perriwig did not prove so strange to the world as I was afeared it would, for I thought that all the church would presently have cast their eyes upon me, but I found no such thing." About his meannesses over money, his jealousies, and his injustices, he penned, "Home and found all well, only myself somewhat vexed at my wife's neglect in leaving her scarfe, waistcoat and night dressings in the coach today; though I confess she did give them to me to look after." He possessed, in a unique degree, the quality of complete honesty. His diary paints not only his own infirmities but the frailty of all mankind.

After the successful publication of Evelyn's diary in 1818, Pepys's diary was transcribed—with great accuracy—by John Smith, later rector of Baldock, Hertfordshire.

The Court Wits

Among the subjects for gossip in London, the group known as the court wits held a special place. Their conduct of their lives provoked censure from many, but among them were poets of some distinction who drew upon the example of gentlemen-authors of the preceding generation, especially Sir John Suckling, Abraham Cowley, and Edmund Waller, the last two of whom themselves survived into the Restoration and continued to write impressive verse.

The court wits' best works are mostly light lyrics; for example, Sir Charles Sedley's "Not, Celia, that I juster am" or Charles Sackville, earl of Dorset's "Dorinda's sparkling wit, and eyes." However, one of their number, John Wilmot, the earl of Rochester, possessed a wider range and richer talent. Though some of his surviving poetry is in the least-ambitious sense occasional work, he also produced writing of great force and authority, including a group of lyrics (for example, "All my past life is mine no more" and "An age in her embraces past") that, in psychological grasp and limpid deftness of phrasing, are among the finest of the century. He also wrote the harsh and scornfully dismissive *Satire Against Reason and Mankind* (probably before 1676), in which, as elsewhere in his verse, his libertinism seems philosophical as well as sexual. He doubts religious truths and sometimes seems to be versifying the scandalous materialism of Thomas Hobbes. Indeed, some of his verse that vaunts its obscenity has an aspect of nihilism, as if the amoral sexual epicure were but fending off fear of oblivion.

More lightly, Rochester experimented ingeniously with various forms of verse satire on contemporary society. The most brilliant of these, *A Letter from Artemisia in the Town, to Chloë in the Country* (written about 1675), combines a shrewd ear for currently fashionable idioms with a

Chinese box structure that masks the author's own thoughts. Rochester's determined use of strategies of indirection anticipates Swift's tactics as an ironist.

John Oldham, a young schoolmaster, received encouragement as a poet from Rochester. His career, like his patron's, was to be cut short by an early death in 1683, at age 30. But of his promise there can be no doubt. (Dryden wrote a fine elegy upon him.) Oldham's *Satires upon the Jesuits* (1681), written during the Popish Plot, makes too unrelenting use of a rancorous, hectoring tone, but his development of the possibilities (especially satiric) of the "imitation" form, already explored by Rochester in, for example, *An Allusion to Horace* (written 1675–76), earns him an honourable place in the history of a mode that Pope was to put to such dazzling use. His imitation of the ninth satire of Horace's first book exemplifies the agility and tonal resource with which Oldham could adapt a Classical original to, and bring its values to bear upon, Restoration experience.

A poet who found early popularity with Restoration readers is Charles Cotton, whose *Scarronides* (1664–65), travesties of Books I and IV of Virgil's *Aeneid*, set a fashion for poetic burlesque. He is valued today, however, for work that attracted less contemporary interest but was to be admired by the Romantics William Wordsworth, Samuel Taylor Coleridge, and Charles Lamb. The posthumous *Poems on Several Occasions* (1689) includes deft poetry of friendship and love written with the familiar, colloquial ease of the Cavalier tradition and carefully observed, idiosyncratically executed descriptions of nature. He also added a second part to his friend Izaak Walton's *The Compleat Angler* in 1676.

A writer whose finest work was unknown to his contemporaries, much of it not published until the 20th century, is the poet and mystic Thomas Traherne.

Influenced by the Hermetic writings attributed to the Egyptian god Thoth and by the lengthy Platonic tradition, he wrote, with extreme transparency of style, out of a conviction of the original innocence and visionary illumination of infancy. His poetry, though uneven, contains some remarkable writing, but his richest achievements are perhaps to be found in the prose *Centuries of Meditations* (first published in 1908).

John Dryden

A poetic accomplishment of quite another order is that of John Dryden. He was 29 years old when Charles II returned from exile, and little writing by him survives from before that date. However, for the remaining 40 years of his life, he was unwearyingly productive, responding to the challenges of an unstable world with great formal originality and a mastery of many poetic styles.

Contemporaries perhaps saw his achievements differently from 21st-century readers. In the early part of his career, he was above all a successful dramatist. He wrote heroic plays in rhyming verse, topical comedies, adaptations of Shakespeare, operas, and subtle tragicomedies. The great achievements of his later career were in the field of translation, especially from Latin. This culminated in his magisterial version of the works of Virgil (1697). His demonstration that English verse could, in some sense, match its Classical models deeply impressed later writers, notably Alexander Pope.

Dryden was profoundly a poet of the public domain, but the ways in which he addressed himself to the issues of the day varied greatly in the course of his career. Thus, his poem to celebrate the Restoration itself, *Astraea Redux* (1660), invokes Roman ideas of the return of a golden age under Augustus Caesar in order to encourage similar hopes

Heroic Play

The heroic play—also called heroic drama or heroic tragedy—is a type of play that was prevalent in Restoration England during the 1660s and 1670s.

Modeled after French Neoclassical tragedy, the heroic play was written in rhyming pentameter couplets. Such plays presented characters of almost superhuman stature, and their predominant themes were exalted ideals of love, honour, and courage. The heroic play was based on the traditional epic and romance. The most popular writer of heroic plays was John Dryden, whose *Conquest of Granada*, in two parts (1670, 1671), had all the requisite elements of poetry, battle, courage, death, and murder. George Villiers, 2nd duke of Buckingham, satirized the heroic play in *The Rehearsal* (first performed 1671), its particular target being Dryden. Although Dryden continued to use the form through the mid-1670s, the heroic play had largely died out as a genre by the end of the decade. The term *heroic play* has also been applied to plays with all the attributes given above, but written in blank verse.

for England's future; whereas in 1681 the Exclusion Crisis drew from Dryden one of his masterpieces, *Absalom and Achitophel*, in which the Old Testament story of King David, through an ingenious mingling of heroic and satiric tones, is made to shadow and comment decisively upon the current political confrontation. Another of his finest inventions, *Mac Flecknoe* (written mid-1670s, published 1682), explores, through agile mock-heroic fantasy, the possibility of a world in which the profession of humane letters has been thoroughly debased through the unworthiness of its practitioners.

The 1680s also saw the publication of two major religious poems: *Religio Laici*; *or, A Layman's Faith* (1682), in which Dryden uses a plain style to handle calmly the basic issues of faith, and *The Hind and the Panther* (1687), in which an elaborate allegorical beast fable is deployed to trace the history of animosities between Anglicanism and Roman Catholicism. In the *Glorious Revolution* (1688) Dryden stayed loyal to the Catholicism to which he had converted a few years earlier and thus lost his public offices. Financial need spurred him into even more literary activity

John Dryden was a prolific writer who was not hemmed in by any particular style of verse. Dryden made a name for himself as a poet, dramatist, and translator. Hulton Archive/Getty Images

Beast Fable

A beast fable is a prose or verse fable or short story that usually has a moral. In beast fables animal characters are represented as acting with human feelings and motives. Among the best-known examples in Western literature are those attributed to the legendary Greek author Aesop. Instances of the genre have been produced throughout the history of English literature, with John Dryden's *The Hind and the Panther* (1687) one of the most prominent from the 17th and 18th centuries.

thereafter, and his last years produced not only his version of Virgil but also immensely skilled translations of Juvenal and Persius, handsome versions of Giovanni Boccaccio and Geoffrey Chaucer, and further fine original poetry.

Dryden was, in addition, in Samuel Johnson's words, the father of English criticism. Throughout his career he wrote extensively on matters of critical precept and poetic practice. Such sustained effort for which there was no precedent not only presumed the possibility of an interested audience but also contributed substantially to the creation of one. His tone is consistently exploratory and undogmatic. He writes as a working author, with an eye to problems he has himself faced, and is skeptical of theoretical prescriptions, even those that seem to come with Classical authority. His discussion of Ben Jonson's *Epicoene; or, The Silent Woman* in *Of Dramatic Poesie, an Essay* (1668) is remarkable as the first extended analysis of an English play, and his *Discourse Concerning the Origin and Progress of Satire* (1693) and the preface to the *Fables Ancient and Modern* (1700) both contain detailed commentary of the highest order.

A contrary critical philosophy was espoused by Thomas Rymer, an adherent of the most-rigid Neoclassical notions of dramatic decorum, who surveyed the pre-1642 English drama in *Tragedies of the Last Age* (1678) and *A Short View of Tragedy* (1693) and found it wanting. His zealotry reads unattractively today, but Dryden was impressed by him, if disinclined to accept his judgments without protest. In due course the post-1660 playwrights were to find their own scourge in Jeremy Collier, whose *A Short View of the Immorality and Profaneness of the English Stage* (1698) comprehensively indicted the Restoration stage tradition. The theoretical frame of Collier's tract is crude, but his strength lay in his dogged citation of evidence from published play texts, especially when the charge was blasphemy, a crime still liable to stiff penalties in the courts. Even so clever a man as the dramatist William Congreve was left struggling when attempting to deny in print the freedoms he had allowed his wit.

Drama by Dryden and Others

As a dramatist, Dryden experimented vigorously in all the popular stage modes of the day, producing some distinguished tragic writing in *All for Love* (1677) and *Don Sebastian* (1689). But his greatest achievement, *Amphitryon* (1690), is a comedy. In this he was typical of his age. Though there were individual successes in tragedy, especially Thomas Otway's *Venice Preserved* (1682) and Nathaniel Lee's *Lucius Junius Brutus* (1680), the splendour of the Restoration theatre lies in its comic creativity.

Several generations of dramatists contributed to that wealth. In the 1670s the most original work can be found in Sir George Etherege's *The Man of Mode* (1676), William Wycherley's *The Country Wife* (1675) and *The Plain Dealer* (1676), and Aphra Behn's two-part *The Rover* (1677, 1681). Commentary has often claimed to detect a disabling repetitiveness in even the best Restoration comic invention, but an attentive reading of *The Country Wife* and *The Man of Mode* will reveal how firmly the two authors, close acquaintances, devised dramatic worlds significantly dissimilar in atmosphere that set distinctive challenges for their players. Both plays were to scandalize future generations with their shared acceptance that the only credible virtues were intelligence and grace, together producing "wit."

The disturbed years of the Popish Plot produced comic writing of matching mood, especially in Otway's abrasive *Soldier's Fortune* (1680) and Lee's extraordinary variation on the Madame de La Fayette novella, *The Princess of Cleve* (1681–82). After the Glorious Revolution a series of major comedies hinged on marital dissension and questions (not unrelated to contemporary political traumas) of contract, breach of promise, and the nature of authority. These include, in addition to *Amphitryon*, Thomas Southerne's *The Wives' Excuse* (1691), Sir John Vanbrugh's *The Relapse* (1696) and *The Provoked Wife* (1697), and George Farquhar's *The Beaux' Stratagem* (1707).

These years also saw the premieres of William Congreve's four comedies and one tragedy, climaxing with his masterpiece, *The Way of the World* (1700), a brilliant combination of intricate plotting and incisively humane portraiture. The pressures brought upon society at home by continental wars against the French also began to make themselves felt, the key text here being Farquhar's *The Recruiting Officer* (1706), in which the worlds of soldier and civilian are placed in suggestive proximity.

CHAPTER 2

THE 18TH CENTURY

One of the most striking qualities of the 18th century in Great Britain was its optimism, and the names given to the period by those living through it and by those who followed attempted to capture its spirit of improvement and progress. Many people of the time thought they were experiencing a golden period similar to that of the Roman emperor Augustus; for this reason the name Augustan was given to the early 18th century. The century has also been called the Age of Enlightenment. The act of looking backward to ancient authors was also given a forward-looking twist. Although many writers of the era used ancient Greek and Roman authors as models of style, they adapted and made these models new, a reworking that drew the label *neoclassical*.

Merchants and tradesmen achieved tremendous economic power during the 18th century, and people who today would be labelled as scientists drew an increasing amount of attention during what has been called the Classic Age of Science. Many important inventions—the spinning jenny, the power loom, and the steam engine, among others—helped to bring about an industrial society. Cities grew in size, and London began to assume a position as a great industrial and commercial center. In addition to a comfortable life, many of the members of the middle class demanded a respectable, moralistic art that was controlled by common sense—or, more precisely, a "common sense" that aligned with their own bourgeois worldview. Theirs was a perspective formed in protest to what they perceived as the aristocratic immoralities in much of the Restoration literature, and its influence would reach throughout the century.

PUBLICATION OF POLITICAL MATERIAL

The expiry of the Licensing Act in 1695 halted state censorship of the press. During the next 20 years there were to be 10 general elections. These two factors combined to produce an enormous growth in the publication of political literature. Senior politicians, especially Robert Harley, saw the potential importance of the pamphleteer in wooing the support of a wavering electorate, and numberless hack writers produced copy for the presses. Richer talents also played their part. Harley, for instance, instigated Daniel Defoe's industrious work on the *Review* (1704–13), which consisted, in essence, of a regular political essay defending, if often by indirection, current governmental policy. He also secured Jonathan Swift's polemical skills for contributions to *The Examiner* (1710–11). Swift's most ambitious intervention in the paper war, again overseen by Harley, was *The Conduct of the Allies* (1711), a devastatingly lucid argument against any further prolongation of the War of the Spanish Succession.

Writers such as Defoe and Swift did not confine themselves to straightforward discursive techniques in their pamphleteering but experimented deftly with mock forms and invented personae to carry the attack home. In doing so, both writers made sometimes mischievous use of the anonymity that was conventional at the time. According to contemporary testimony, one of Defoe's anonymous works, *The Shortest-Way with the Dissenters* (1702), so

Recognizing the persuasive power of a well-written essay, statesman Robert Harley enlisted the assistance of Jonathan Swift to wield his pen in a "paper war" against policies of the sitting government. Hulton Archive/Getty Images

brilliantly sustained its impersonation of a High Church extremist, its supposed narrator, that it was at first mistaken for the real thing. Anonymity was to be an important creative resource for Defoe in his novels and for Swift in his prose satires.

PERIODICAL JOURNALISM

The avalanche of political writing whetted the contemporary appetite for reading matter generally and, in the increasing sophistication of its ironic and fictional maneuvers, assisted in preparing the way for the astonishing growth in popularity of narrative fiction during the subsequent decades. It also helped fuel the other great new genre of the 18th century—periodical journalism.

After Defoe's *Review,* the great innovation in this field came with the achievements of Richard Steele and Joseph Addison in *The Tatler* (1709–11) and then *The Spectator* (1711–12). In a familiar, urbane style they tackled a great range of topics, from politics to fashion, from aesthetics to the development of commerce. They aligned themselves with those who wished to see a purification of manners after the laxity of the Restoration and wrote extensively, with descriptive and reformative intent, about social and family relations. Their political allegiances were Whig, and in their creation of Sir Roger de Coverley they painted a wry portrait of the landed Tory squire as likable, possessed of good qualities, but feckless and anachronistic. Contrariwise, they spoke admiringly of the positive and honourable virtues bred by a healthy, and expansionist, mercantile community.

Addison, the more original of the two, was an adventurous literary critic who encouraged esteem for the ballad through his enthusiastic account of *Chevy Chase* and hymned the pleasures of the imagination in a series of papers deeply influential on 18th-century thought. His long, thoughtful, and probing examen of John Milton's *Paradise Lost* played a major role in establishing the poem as the great epic of English literature and as a source of religious wisdom. The success with which Addison and Steele established the periodical essay as a prestigious form can be judged by the fact that they were to have more than 300 imitators before the end of the century. The awareness of their society and curiosity about the way it was developing, which they encouraged in their eager and diverse readership, left its mark on much subsequent writing.

The Tatler and *The Spectator*

The Tatler was a periodical launched in London by the essayist Sir Richard Steele in April 1709, appearing three times weekly until January 1711. At first its avowed intention was to present accounts of gallantry, pleasure, and entertainment, of poetry, and of foreign and domestic news. These all were reported and "issued" from various London coffee and chocolate houses. In time *The Tatler* began to investigate manners and society, establishing its principles of ideal behaviour, its concepts of a pefect gentleman and gentlewoman, and its standards of good taste. Dueling, gambling, rakish behaviour, and coquettishness were criticized, and virtuous action was admired. Numerous anecdotes and stories gave point to the moral codes advanced. The periodical had an explicit Whig allegiance and was several times drawn into political controversy.

The English periodical essay began its first flowering in *The Tatler*, reaching its full bloom in the hands of Joseph Addison, who seems to have made his first contribution to the periodical in the 18th issue. Two months after *The Tatler* ceased publication, he and Steele launched a brilliant new periodical. *The Spectator* was published in London from March 1, 1711, to Dec. 6, 1712 (appearing daily), and subsequently revived by Addison in 1714 (for 80 numbers).

In its aim to "enliven morality with wit, and to temper wit with morality," *The Spectator* adopted a fictional method of presentation through a "Spectator Club," whose imaginary members extolled the authors' own ideas about society. These "members" included representatives of commerce, the army, the town (respectively, Sir Andrew Freeport, Captain Sentry, and Will Honeycomb), and of the country gentry (Sir Roger de Coverley). The papers were ostensibly written by Mr. Spectator, an "observer" of the London scene. The conversations that *The Spectator* reported were often imagined to take place in coffeehouses, which was also where many copies of the publication were distributed and read.

Though Whiggish in tone, *The Spectator* generally avoided party-political controversy. An important aspect of its success was its notion that urbanity and taste were values that transcended political differences. Almost immediately it was

THE

SPECTATOR.

VOLUME the FIRST.

LONDON:

Printed for J. and R. TONSON and S. DRAPE[R]

The title page of the collected edition of The Spectator, Vol. 1. *The essays and articles from the periodical's nearly two-year first run were collected and sold in seven individual volumes.* Private Collection/ The Bridgeman Art Library

hugely admired. Mr. Spectator had, observed the poet and dramatist John Gay, "come on like a Torrent and swept all before him."

Because of its fictional framework, *The Spectator* is sometimes said to have heralded the rise of the English novel in the 18th century. This is perhaps an overstatement, since the fictional framework, once adopted, ceased to be of primary importance and served instead as a social microcosm within which a tone at once grave, good-humoured, and flexible could be sounded. The real authors of the essays were free to consider whatever topics they pleased, with reference to the fictional framework (as in Steele's account of Sir Roger's views on marriage, which appeared in issue no. 113) or without it (as in Addison's critical papers on *Paradise Lost*, John Milton's epic poem, which appeared in issues no. 267, 273, and others).

Given the success of *The Spectator* in promoting an ideal of polite sociability, the correspondence of its supposed readers was an important feature of the publication. These letters may or may not, on occasion, have been composed by the editors.

In addition to Addison and Steele themselves, contributors included Alexander Pope, Thomas Tickell, and Ambrose Philips. Addison's reputation as an essayist has surpassed that of Steele, but their individual contributions to the success of *The Spectator* are less to the point than their collaborative efforts. Steele's friendly tone was a perfect balance and support for the more dispassionate style of Addison. Their joint achievement was to lift serious discussion from the realms of religious and political partisanship and to make it instead a normal pastime of the leisured class. Together they set the pattern and established the vogue for the periodical throughout the rest of the century and helped to create a receptive public for the novelists, ensuring that the new kind of prose writing—however entertaining—should be essentially serious.

Later in the century other periodical forms developed. Edward Cave invented the idea of the "magazine," founding the hugely successful *Gentleman's Magazine* in 1731. One of its most prolific early contributors was the young Samuel Johnson. Periodical writing was a major part of Johnson's career, as it was for writers such as Henry Fielding and Oliver Goldsmith. The practice and the status of criticism were transformed in mid-century by the *Monthly Review* (founded 1749) and the *Critical Review* (founded 1756). The latter was edited by Tobias Smollett. From this period the influence of reviews began to shape literary output, and writers began to acknowledge their importance.

MAJOR POLITICAL WRITERS

The controversy over who would succeed Queen Anne—resolved, somewhat uneasily, by the Act of Settlement (1701) and the subsequent assumption of the British throne by a foreign-born king—produced a unsettled, vitriolic political environment in England. The union of England and Scotland, forged through the Act of Union of 1707, created the entity known as Great Britain—a new governmental structure that itself created new political and personal identities for the citizens of the joined kingdoms. These two events reverberated throughout a century that would witness many more large-scale political changes and that would eventually give rise, in the 1790s, to the destructive outbreak of the French revolutionary and Napoleonic wars, which swept across much of Europe.

To write poetry or prose amidst these world-changing events was to engage, explicitly or not, with the political environment of the age. Every writer, it might be argued, was a political writer. Some, such as Alexander Pope, James Thompson, and Jonathan Swift, were simply more forthright about their subject matter than others.

Alexander Pope

Alexander Pope contributed to *The Spectator* and moved for a time in Addisonian circles. But from about 1711 onward, his more-influential friendships were with Tory intellectuals. Pope's view of the transformations wrought

Alexander Pope, portrait by Thomas Hudson; in the National Portrait Gallery, London. Courtesy of the National Portrait Gallery, London

in Robert Walpole's England by economic individualism and opportunism grew increasingly embittered and despairing. In this he was following a common Tory trend, which is reflected in his later writing.

Pope's upbringing, particularly his religion, were to play an important part in his writing and political affiliations. His father, a wholesale linen merchant, retired from business in 1688, the year of his son's birth, and in 1700 went to live at Binfield in Windsor Forest. The Popes were Roman Catholics, and at Binfield they came to know several neighbouring Catholic families who were to play an important part in the poet's life. Pope's religion procured him some lifelong friends, notably Martha Blount, to whom Pope addressed some of the most memorable of his poems and to whom he bequeathed most of his property.

But his religion also precluded him from a formal course of education, since Catholics were not admitted to the universities. He was trained at home by Catholic priests for a short time and attended Catholic schools at Twyford, near Winchester, and at Hyde Park Corner, London, but he was mainly self-educated. He was a precocious boy, eagerly reading Latin, Greek, French, and Italian, which he managed to teach himself, and an incessant scribbler, turning out verse upon verse in imitation of the poets he read. The best of these early writings are the *Ode on Solitude* and a paraphrase of St. Thomas à Kempis, both of which he claimed to have written at age 12.

Works, Homer and *The Dunciad*

Windsor Forest was near enough to London to permit Pope's frequent visits there. He early grew acquainted with former members of John Dryden's circle, notably William Wycherley, William Walsh, and Henry Cromwell.

By 1705 his *Pastorals* were in draft and were circulating among the best literary judges of the day. In 1706 Jacob Tonson, the leading publisher of poetry, had solicited their publication, and they took the place of honour in his *Poetical Miscellanies* in 1709.

When the *Pastorals* were published, Pope was already at work on a poem on the art of writing. This was *An Essay on Criticism*, published in 1711. Its brilliantly polished epigrams (e.g., "A little learning is a dangerous thing," "To err is human, to forgive, divine," and "For fools rush in where angels fear to tread"), which have become part of the proverbial heritage of the language, are readily traced to their sources in Horace, Quintilian, Boileau, and other critics, ancient and modern, in verse and prose. Yet the charge that the poem is derivative, so often made in the past, takes insufficient account of Pope's success in harmonizing a century of conflict in critical thinking and in showing how nature may best be mirrored in art.

The well-deserved success of *An Essay on Criticism* brought Pope a wider circle of friends, notably Richard Steele and Joseph Addison, who were then collaborating on *The Spectator*. To this journal Pope contributed the most original of his pastorals, *The Messiah* (1712), and perhaps other papers in prose. He was clearly influenced by *The Spectator*'s policy of correcting public morals by witty admonishment, and in this vein he wrote the first version of his mock epic, *The Rape of the Lock* (two cantos, 1712; five cantos, 1714), to reconcile two Catholic families. A young man in one family had stolen a lock of hair from a young lady in the other. Pope treated the dispute that followed as though it were comparable to the mighty quarrel between Greeks and Trojans, which had been Homer's theme.

Telling the story with all the pomp and circumstance of epic made not only the participants in the quarrel but also the society in which they lived seem ridiculous. Though it was a society where

. . . Britain's statesmen oft the fall foredoom
Of foreign tyrants, and of nymphs at home

as if one occupation concerned them as much as the other, and though in such a society a young lady might do equally ill to

. . . stain her honour, or her new brocade;
Forget her pray'rs, or miss a masquerade.

Pope managed also to suggest what genuine attractions existed amid the foppery. It is a glittering poem about a glittering world. He acknowledged how false the sense of values was that paid so much attention to external appearance, but ridicule and rebuke slide imperceptibly into admiration and tender affection as the heroine, Belinda, is conveyed along the Thames to Hampton Court, the scene of the "rape":

But now secure the painted vessel glides,
The sunbeams trembling on the floating tides:
While melting music steals upon the sky,
And soften'd sounds along the waters die;
Smooth flow the waves, the zephyrs gently play,
Belinda smil'd, and all the world was gay.

A comparable blend of seemingly incompatible responses—love and hate, bawdiness and decorum, admiration and ridicule—is to be found in all Pope's later satires. The poem is thick with witty allusions to classical verse and, notably, to Milton's *Paradise Lost*. The art of allusion is an element of much of Pope's poetry.

Pope had also been at work for several years on *Windsor-Forest*. In this poem, completed and published in 1713, he proceeded, as Virgil had done, from the pastoral vein to the georgic and celebrated the rule of Queen Anne as the Latin poet had celebrated the rule of Augustus. In another early poem, *Eloisa to Abelard*, Pope borrowed the form of Ovid's "heroic epistle" (in which an abandoned lady addresses her lover) and showed imaginative skill in conveying the struggle between sexual passion and dedication to a life of celibacy.

These poems and other works were collected in the first volume of Pope's *Works* in 1717. When it was published, he was already far advanced with the greatest labour of his life, his verse translation of Homer. He had announced his intentions in October 1713 and had published the first volume, containing the *Iliad*, Books I–IV, in 1715. The *Iliad* was completed in six volumes in 1720. The work of translating the *Odyssey* (vol. i–iii, 1725; vol. iv and v, 1726) was shared with William Broome, who had contributed notes to the *Iliad*, and Elijah Fenton. The labour had been great, but so were the rewards. By the two translations Pope cleared about £10,000 and was able to claim that, thanks to Homer, he could ". . . live and thrive / Indebted to no Prince or Peer alive."

The merits of Pope's Homer lie less in the accuracy of translation and in correct representation of the spirit of the original than in the achievement of a heroic poem as his contemporaries understood it: a poem Virgilian in its dignity, moral purpose, and pictorial splendour, yet one that consistently kept Homer in view and alluded to him throughout. Pope offered his readers the *Iliad* and the *Odyssey* as he felt sure Homer would have written them had he lived in early 18th-century England.

Political considerations had affected the success of the translation. As a Roman Catholic, he had Tory affiliations rather than Whig. Though he retained the friendship of such Whigs as William Congreve, Nicholas Rowe, and the painter Charles Jervas, his ties with Steele and Addison grew strained as a result of the political animosity that occurred at the end of Queen Anne's reign. He found new and lasting friends in Tory circles—Jonathan Swift, John Gay, John Arbuthnot, Thomas Parnell, the earl of Oxford, and Viscount Bolingbroke. He was associated with the first five in the Scriblerus Club (1713–14), which met to write joint satires on pedantry, later to mature as *Peri Bathouse; or, The Art of Sinking in Poetry* (1728) and the *Memoirs of Martinus Scriblerus* (1741). These were the men who encouraged his translation of Homer. The Whigs, who associated with Addison at Button's Coffee-House, put up a rival translator in Thomas Tickell, who published his version of the *Iliad*, Book I, two days after Pope's. Addison preferred Tickell's manifestly inferior version. His praise increased the resentment Pope already felt because of a series of slights and misunderstandings. When Pope heard gossip of further malice on Addison's part, he sent him a satiric view of his character, published later as the character of Atticus, the insincere arbiter of literary taste in *An Epistle to Dr. Arbuthnot* (1735).

Even before the Homer quarrel, Pope had found that the life of a wit was one of perpetual warfare. There were few years when either his person or his poems were not objects of attacks from the critic John Dennis, the bookseller Edmund Curll, the historian John Oldmixon, and other writers of lesser fame. The climax was reached over his edition of Shakespeare. He had emended the plays, in the spirit of a literary editor, to accord with contemporary taste (1725), but his practice was exposed by the scholar Lewis Theobald in *Shakespeare Restored* (1726).

Though Pope had ignored some of these attacks, he had replied to others with squibs in prose and verse. But he now attempted to make an end of the opposition and to defend his standards, which he aligned with the standards of civilized society, in the mock epic *The Dunciad* (1728). Theobald was represented in it as the Goddess of Dullness's favourite son, a suitable hero for those leaden times, and others who had given offense were preserved like flies in amber. Pope dispatches his victims with such sensuousness of verse and imagery that the reader is forced to admit that if there is petulance here, as has often been claimed, it is, to parody Wordsworth, petulance recollected in tranquillity. Pope reissued the poem in 1729 with an elaborate mock commentary of prefaces, notes, appendixes, indexes, and errata. This burlesque of pedantry whimsically suggested that *The Dunciad* had fallen a victim to the spirit of the times and been edited by a dunce.

Later Life and Influence

Pope now began to contemplate a new work on the relations of man, nature, and society that would be a grand organization of human experience and intuition, but he was destined never to complete it. *An Essay on Man* (1733–34) was intended as an introductory book discussing the overall design of this work. The poem has often been charged with shallowness and philosophical inconsistency, and there is indeed little that is original in its thought, almost all of which can be traced in the work of the great thinkers of Western civilization. Subordinate themes were treated in greater detail in *Of the Use of Riches, an Epistle to Bathurst* (1732), *An Epistle to Cobham, of the Knowledge and Characters of Men* (1733), and *Of the Characters of Women: An Epistle to a Lady* (1735).

Pope was deflected from this "system of ethics in the Horatian way" by the renewed need for self-defense. Critical attacks drove him to consider his position as satirist. He chose to adapt for his own defense the first satire of Horace's second book, where the ethics of satire are propounded, and, after discussing the question in correspondence with Dr. John Arbuthnot, he addressed to him an epistle in verse (1735), one of the finest of his later poems, in which were incorporated fragments written over several years. His case in *An Epistle to Dr. Arbuthnot* was a traditional one: that depravity in public morals had roused him to stigmatize outstanding offenders beyond the reach of the law, concealing the names of some and representing others as types, and that he was innocent of personal rancour and habitually forbearing under attack.

The success of his *First Satire of the Second Book of Horace, Imitated* (1733) led to the publication (1734–38) of 10 more of these paraphrases of Horatian themes adapted to the contemporary social and political scene. Pope's poems followed Horace's satires and epistles sufficiently closely for him to print the Latin on facing pages with the English, but whoever chose to make the comparison would notice a continuous enrichment of the original by parenthetic thrusts and compliments, as well as by the freshness of the imagery. The series was concluded with two dialogues in verse, republished as the *Epilogue to the Satires* (1738), where, as in *An Epistle to Dr. Arbuthnot*, Pope ingeniously combined a defense of his own career and character with a restatement of the satirist's traditional apology.

In these imitations and dialogues, Pope directed his attack upon the materialistic standards of the commercially minded Whigs in power and upon the corrupting effect of money, while restating and illustrating the old Horatian standards of serene and temperate living. His anxiety about prevailing standards was shown once more in his last completed work, *The New Dunciad* (1742), reprinted as the fourth book of a revised *Dunciad* (1743), in which Theobald was replaced as hero by Colley Cibber, the poet laureate and actor-manager, who not only had given more recent cause of offense but seemed a more appropriate representative of the degenerate standards of the age. In *Dunciad,* Book IV, the Philistine culture of the city of London was seen to overtake the court and seat of government at Westminster, and the poem ends in a magnificent but baleful prophecy of anarchy. Pope had begun work on *Brutus,* an epic poem in blank verse, and on a revision of his poems for a new edition, but neither was complete at his death in 1744.

Pope's favourite metre was the 10-syllable iambic pentameter rhyming (heroic) couplet. He handled it with increasing skill and adapted it to such varied purposes as the epigrammatic summary of *An Essay on Criticism*, the pathos of *Verses to the Memory of an Unfortunate Lady*, the mock heroic of *The Rape of the Lock*, the discursive tones of *An Essay on Man*, the rapid narrative of the Homer translation, and the Miltonic sublimity of the conclusion of *The Dunciad.* But his greatest triumphs of versification are found in the *Epilogue to the Satires*, where he moves easily from witty, spirited dialogue to noble and elevated declamation, and in *An Epistle to Dr. Arbuthnot*, which opens with a scene of domestic irritation suitably conveyed in broken rhythm:

Shut, shut the door, good John! fatigu'd, I said:
Tie up the knocker, say I'm sick, I'm dead.
The Dog-star rages! nay 'tis past a doubt,
All Bedlam, or Parnassus, is let out:
Fire in each eye, and papers in each hand,
They rave, recite, and madden round the land;

The poem closes with a deliberately chosen contrast of domestic calm, which the poet may be said to have deserved and won during the course of the poem:

Me, let the tender office long engage
To rock the cradle of reposing age,
With lenient arts extend a mother's breath,
Make languor smile, and smooth the bed of death,
Explore the thought, explain the asking eye,
And keep a while one parent from the sky!

Pope's command of diction is no less happily adapted to his theme and to the type of poem, and the range of his imagery is remarkably wide. He has been thought defective in imaginative power, but this opinion cannot be sustained in view of the invention and organizing ability shown notably in *The Rape of the Lock* and *The Dunciad*. He was the first English poet to enjoy contemporary fame in France and Italy and throughout the European continent and to see translations of his poems into modern as well as ancient languages.

Thomson, Prior, and Gay

Like Pope, James Thomson also sided with the opposition to Walpole, but his poetry sustained a much more optimistic vision. In *The Seasons* (first published as a complete entity in 1730 but then massively revised and expanded until 1746), Thomson meditated upon and described with fascinated precision the phenomena of nature. He brought to the task a vast array of erudition and a delighted absorption in the discoveries of post–Civil War science (especially Newtonian science), from whose vocabulary he borrowed freely. The image he developed of man's relationship to, and cultivation of, nature provided a buoyant portrait of the achieved civilization and wealth that ultimately derive from them and that, in his judgment, contemporary England enjoyed. The diction of *The Seasons*, which is written in blank verse, has many Miltonian echoes. In *The Castle of Indolence* (1748) Thomson's model is Spenserian, and its wryly developed allegory lauds the virtues of industriousness and mercantile achievement.

A poet who wrote less ambitiously but with a special urbanity is Matthew Prior, a diplomat and politician of some distinction, who essayed graver themes in *Solomon on the Vanity of the World* (1718), a disquisition on the vanity of human knowledge, but who also wrote some of the most direct and coolly elegant love poetry of the period. Prior's principal competitor as a writer of light verse was John Gay, whose *Trivia; or, The Art of Walking the Streets of London* (1716) catalogues the dizzying diversity of urban life through a dexterous burlesque of Virgil's *Georgics*. His *Fables*, particularly those in the 1738 collection, contain sharp, subtle writing, and his work for the stage, especially in *The What D'Ye Call It* (1715), *Three Hours After Marriage* (1717; written with John Arbuthnot and Pope), and *The Beggar's Opera* (1728), shows a sustained ability to breed original and vital effects from witty generic cross-fertilization.

Swift

Jonathan Swift, who was born in 1667 in Dublin, wrote both poetry and prose throughout his career. Like Gay, he favoured octosyllabic couplets and a close mimicry of the movement of colloquial speech. His technical virtuosity allowed him to switch assuredly from poetry of great destructive force to the intricately textured humour of *Verses on the Death of Dr. Swift* (completed in 1732; published 1739) and to the delicate humanity of his poems to

Stella. But his prime distinction is as the greatest prose satirist in the English language. His period in the 1690s as secretary to the distinguished man of letters Sir William Temple gave him the chance to extend and consolidate his reading.

Jonathan Swift's reputation as a political satirist was firmly entrenched even before the publication of Gulliver's Travels, *the book for which he is best known.* Hulton Archive/Getty Images

Between 1691 and 1694 Swift wrote a number of poems, notably six odes. But his true genius did not find expression until he turned from verse to prose satire and composed, mostly at Moor Park between 1696 and 1699, *A Tale of a Tub*, one of his major works. Published anonymously in 1704, this work was made up of three associated pieces: the *Tale* itself, a satire against "the numerous and gross corruptions in religion and learning"; the mock-heroic *Battle of the Books*; and the *Discourse Concerning the Mechanical Operation of the Spirit*, which ridiculed the manner of worship and preaching of religious enthusiasts at that period. In the *Battle of the Books*, Swift supports the ancients in the longstanding dispute about the relative merits of ancient versus modern literature and culture. But *A Tale of a Tub* is the most impressive of the three compositions. This work is outstanding for its exuberance of satiric wit and energy and is marked by an incomparable command of stylistic effects, largely in the nature of parody. Swift saw the realm of culture and literature threatened by zealous pedantry, while religion—which for him meant rational Anglicanism—suffered attack from both Roman Catholicism and the Nonconformist (Dissenting) churches. In the *Tale* he proceeded to trace all these dangers to a single source: the irrationalities that disturb man's highest faculties—reason and common sense.

Satirist, Journalist, and Churchman

After Temple's death in 1699, Swift returned to Dublin as chaplain and secretary to the earl of Berkeley, who was then going to Ireland as a lord justice. During the ensuing years he was in England on some four occasions—in 1701, 1702, 1703, and 1707 to 1709—and won wide recognition in London for his intelligence and his wit as a writer. He had resigned his position as vicar of Kilroot, but early in 1700 he was preferred to several posts in the Irish church.

His public writings of this period show that he kept in close touch with affairs in both Ireland and England. Among them is the essay *Discourse of the Contests and Dissensions between the Nobles and the Commons in Athens and Rome*, in which Swift defended the English constitutional balance of power between the monarchy and the two houses of Parliament as a bulwark against tyranny. In London he became increasingly well known through several works: his religious and political essays, *A Tale of a Tub*, and certain impish works, including the "Bickerstaff" pamphlets of 1708–09, which put an end to the career of John Partridge, a popular astrologer, by first prophesying his death and then describing it in circumstantial detail. Like all Swift's satirical works, these pamphlets were published anonymously and were exercises in impersonation. Their supposed author was "Isaac Bickerstaff." For many of the first readers, the very authorship of the satires was a matter for puzzle and speculation.

Swift's works brought him to the attention of a circle of Whig writers led by Joseph Addison, but Swift was uneasy about many policies of the Whig administration. He was a Whig by birth, education, and political principle, but he was also passionately loyal to the Anglican church, and he came to view with apprehension the Whigs' growing determination to yield ground to the Nonconformists. He also frequently mimicked and mocked the proponents of "free thinking": intellectual skeptics who questioned Anglican orthodoxy. A brilliant and still-perplexing example of this is *Argument Against Abolishing Christianity* (1708).

A momentous period began for Swift when in 1710 he once again found himself in London. A Tory ministry headed by Robert Harley (later earl of Oxford) and Henry St. John (later Viscount Bolingbroke) was replacing that of the Whigs. The new administration, bent on bringing hostilities with France to a conclusion, was also assuming a more protective attitude toward the Church of England. Swift's reactions to such a rapidly changing world are vividly recorded in his *Journal to Stella*, a series of letters written between his arrival in England in 1710 and 1713, which he addressed to Esther Johnson and her companion, Rebecca Dingley, who were now living in Dublin. The astute Harley made overtures to Swift and won him over to the Tories. But Swift did not thereby renounce his essentially Whiggish convictions regarding the nature of government. The old Tory theory of the divine right of kings had no claim upon him. The ultimate power, he insisted, derived from the people as a whole and, in the English constitution, had come to be exercised jointly by king, lords, and commons.

Swift quickly became the Tories' chief pamphleteer and political writer and, by the end of October 1710, had taken over the Tory journal, *The Examiner*, which he continued to edit until June 14, 1711. He then began preparing a pamphlet in support of the Tory drive for peace with France. This, *The Conduct of the Allies*, appeared on Nov. 27, 1711, some weeks before the motion in favour of a peace was finally carried in Parliament. Swift was rewarded for his services in April 1713 with his appointment as dean of St. Patrick's Cathedral in Dublin.

With the death of Queen Anne in August 1714 and the accession of George I, the Tories were a ruined party, and Swift's career in England was at an end. He withdrew to Ireland, where he was to pass most of the remainder of his life. After a period of seclusion in his deanery, Swift gradually regained his energy. He turned again to verse, which he continued to write throughout the 1720s and early 1730s, producing the impressive poem *Verses on the Death of Doctor Swift*, among others. By 1720 he was also showing a renewed interest in public affairs. In his Irish pamphlets of this period he came to grips with many of the problems, social and economic, then confronting Ireland. His tone and manner varied from direct factual presentation to exhortation, humour, and bitter irony. Swift blamed Ireland's backward state chiefly on the blindness of the English government; but he also insistently called attention to the things that the Irish themselves might do in order to better their lot.

Of his Irish writings, the *Drapier's Letters* (1724–25) and *A Modest Proposal* are the best known. The first is a series of letters attacking the English government for its scheme to supply Ireland with copper halfpence and farthings. *A Modest Proposal* is a grimly ironic letter of advice in which a public-spirited citizen suggests that Ireland's overpopulation and dire economic conditions could be alleviated if the babies of poor Irish parents were sold as edible delicacies to be eaten by the rich. Both were published anonymously.

Gulliver's Travels

Swift's greatest satire, *Gulliver's Travels*, was published in 1726. It is uncertain when he began this work, but it appears from his correspondence that he was writing in earnest by 1721 and had finished the whole by August 1725. Its success was immediate. Then, and since, it has succeeded in entertaining (and intriguing) all classes of readers. It was completed at a time when he was close to the poet Alexander Pope and the poet and dramatist John Gay. He had been a fellow member of their Scriblerus Club since 1713, and through their correspondence, Pope continued to be one of his most important connections to England.

Swift's masterpiece was originally published without its author's name under the title *Travels into Several Remote Nations of the World*. This work, which is told in Gulliver's "own words," is the most brilliant as well as the most bitter and controversial of his satires. In each of its four books the hero, Lemuel Gulliver, embarks on a voyage; but shipwreck or some other hazard usually casts him up on a strange land. Book I takes him to Lilliput, where he wakes to find himself the giant prisoner of the

The titular character of Gulliver's Travels *endears himself to the Lilliputians, a race of beings who, in Swift's satiric view, represent the pugilistic and egotistical side of human nature.* Hulton Archive/Getty Images

six-inch-high Lilliputians. Man-Mountain, as Gulliver is called, ingratiates himself with the arrogant, self-important Lilliputians when he wades into the sea and captures an invasion fleet from neighbouring Blefescu; but he falls into disfavour when he puts out a fire in the empress' palace by urinating on it. Learning of a plot to charge him with treason, he escapes from the island.

Book II takes Gulliver to Brobdingnag, where the inhabitants are giants. He is cared for kindly by a nine-year-old girl, Glumdalclitch, but his tiny size exposes him to dangers and indignities, such as getting his head caught in a squalling baby's mouth. Also, the giants' small physical imperfections (such as large pores) are highly visible and disturbing to him. Picked up by an eagle and dropped into the sea, he manages to return home.

In Book III Gulliver visits the floating island of Laputa, whose absent-minded inhabitants are so preoccupied with higher speculations that they are in constant danger of accidental collisions. He visits the Academy of Lagado (a travesty of England's Royal Society), where he finds its lunatic savants engaged in such impractical studies as reducing human excrement to the original food. In Luggnagg he meets the Struldbruggs, a race of immortals, whose eternal senility is brutally described.

Book IV takes Gulliver to the Utopian land of the Houyhnhnms—grave, rational, and virtuous horses. There is also another race on the island, uneasily tolerated and used for menial services by the Houyhnhnms. These are the vicious and physically disgusting Yahoos. Although Gulliver pretends at first not to recognize them, he is forced at last to admit the Yahoos are human beings. He finds perfect happiness with the Houyhnhnms, but as he is only a more advanced Yahoo, he is rejected by them in general assembly and is returned to England, where he finds himself no longer able to tolerate the society of his fellow human beings.

Gulliver's Travels's matter-of-fact style and its air of sober reality confer on it an ironic depth that defeats over-simple explanations. Is it essentially comic, or is it a misanthropic depreciation of mankind? Swift certainly seems to use the various races and societies Gulliver encounters in his travels to satirize many of the errors, follies, and frailties that human beings are prone to. The warlike, disputatious, but essentially trivial Lilliputians in Book I and the deranged, impractical pedants and intellectuals in Book III are shown as imbalanced beings lacking common sense and even decency. The Houyhnhnms, by contrast, are the epitome of reason and virtuous simplicity, but Gulliver's own proud identification with these horses and his subsequent disdain for his fellow humans indicates that he too has become imbalanced, and that human beings are simply incapable of aspiring to the virtuous rationality that Gulliver has glimpsed.

LEGACY

The closing years of Swift's life have been the subject of some misrepresentation, and stories have been told of his ungovernable temper and lack of self-control. It has been suggested that he was insane. From youth he had suffered from what is now known to have been Ménière disease, an affliction of the semicircular canals of the ears, causing periods of dizziness and nausea. But his mental powers were in no way affected, and he remained active throughout most of the 1730s—Dublin's foremost citizen and Ireland's great patriot dean. In the autumn of 1739 a great celebration was held in his honour. He had, however, begun to fail physically and later suffered a paralytic stroke, with subsequent aphasia. In 1742 he was declared incapable of caring for himself, and guardians were appointed. After his death, on Oct. 19, 1745, he was buried in St. Patrick's Cathedral. On his memorial tablet is an epitaph of his own composition, which says that he lies "where savage indignation can no longer tear his heart."

Swift's intellectual roots lay in the rationalism that was characteristic of late 17th-century England. This rationalism, with its strong moral sense, its emphasis on common sense, and its distrust of emotionalism, gave him the standards by which he appraised human conduct. At the same time, however, he provided a unique description of reason's weakness and of its use by men and women to delude themselves. His moral principles are scarcely original; his originality lies rather in the quality of his satiric imagination and his literary art. Swift's literary tone varies from the humorous to the savage, but each of his satiric compositions is marked by concentrated power and directness of impact. His command of a great variety of prose styles is unfailing, as is his power of inventing imaginary episodes and all their accompanying details. Swift rarely speaks in his own person; almost always he states his views by ironic indiscretion through some imagined character like Lemuel Gulliver or the morally obtuse citizen of *A Modest Proposal*. Thus Swift's descriptive passages reflect the minds that are describing just as much as the things described. Pulling in different directions, this irony creates the tensions that are characteristic of Swift's best work, and reflects his vision of humanity's ambiguous position between bestiality and reasonableness.

Shaftesbury and Others

Doctrine more consoling than what Swift was able to provide was available in the popular writings of Anthony

Ashley Cooper, 3rd earl of Shaftesbury, which were gathered in his *Characteristics of Men, Manners, Opinions, Times* (1711). Although Shaftesbury had been tutored by Locke, he dissented from the latter's rejection of innate ideas and posited that man is born with a moral sense that is closely associated with his sense of aesthetic form. The tone of Shaftesbury's essays is characteristically idealistic, benevolent, gently reasonable, and unmistakably aristocratic. Yet they were more controversial than now seems likely: such religion as is present there is Deistic, and the philosopher seems warmer toward pagan than Christian wisdom.

His optimism was buffeted by Bernard de Mandeville, whose *Fable of the Bees* (1714–29), which includes *The Grumbling Hive; or, Knaves Turn'd Honest* (1705), takes a closer look at early capitalist society than Shaftesbury was prepared to do. Mandeville stressed the indispensable role played by the ruthless pursuit of self-interest in securing society's prosperous functioning. He thus favoured an altogether harsher view of man's natural instincts than Shaftesbury did and used his formidable gifts as a controversialist to oppose the various contemporary hypocrisies, philosophical and theological, that sought to deny the truth as he saw it. Indeed, he is less a philosopher than a satirist of the philosophies of others, ruthlessly skewering unevidenced optimism and merely theoretical schemes of virtue.

He was, in his turn, the target of acerbic rebukes by, among others, William Law, John Dennis, and Francis Hutcheson. George Berkeley, who criticized both Mandeville and Shaftesbury, set himself against what he took to be the age's irreligious tendencies and the obscurantist defiance by some of his philosophical forbears of the truths of common sense. His *Treatise Concerning the Principles of Human Knowledge* (1710) and *Three Dialogues*

Between Hylas and Philonous (1713) continued the 17th-century debates about the nature of human perception, to which René Descartes and John Locke had contributed. The extreme lucidity and elegance of his style contrast markedly with the more-effortful but intensely earnest prose of Joseph Butler's *Analogy of Religion* (1736), which also seeks to confront contemporary skepticism and ponders scrupulously the bases of man's knowledge of his creator.

In a series of works beginning with *A Treatise of Human Nature* (1739–40), David Hume identified himself as a key spokesman for ironic skepticism and probed uncompromisingly the human mind's propensity to work by sequences of association and juxtaposition rather than by reason. He uniquely merged intellectual rigour with stylistic elegance, writing many beautifully turned essays, including the lengthy, highly successful *History of Great Britain* (1754–62) and his piercingly skeptical *Dialogues Concerning Natural Religion*, published posthumously in 1779. Edmund Burke's *A Philosophical Enquiry into the Origin of Our Ideas of the Sublime and Beautiful* (1757) merged psychological and aesthetic questioning by hypothesizing that the spectator's or reader's delight in the sublime depended upon a sensation of pleasurable pain. An equally bold assumption about human psychology—in this case, that man is an ambitious, socially oriented, product-valuing creature—lies at the heart of Adam Smith's masterpiece of laissez-faire economic theory, *An Inquiry into the Nature and Causes of the Wealth of Nations* (1776). Smith was a friend of Hume's, and both were, with others such as Hutcheson, William Robertson, and Adam Ferguson, part of the Scottish Enlightenment—a flowering of intellectual life centred in Edinburgh and Glasgow in the second half of the 18th century.

MAJOR NOVELISTS

Such ambitious debates on society and human nature ran parallel with the explorations of a literary form finding new popularity with a large audience, the novel.

Daniel Defoe

Daniel Defoe came to sustained prose fiction late in a career of quite various, often disputatious writing. The variety of interests that he had pursued in all his occasional work (much of which is not attributed to him with any certainty) left its mark on his more-lasting achievements. His distinction, though earned in other fields of writing than the polemical, is constantly underpinned by the generous range of his curiosity. Only someone of his catholic interests could have sustained, for instance, the superb *Tour Thro' the Whole Island of Great Britain* (1724–27). This is a vivid county-by-county review and celebration of the state of the nation, which combines an antiquarian's enthusiasm with a passion for trade and commercial progress. He brought the same diversity of enthusiasms into play in writing his novels.

Defoe achieved literary immortality when in 1719 he turned his talents to an extended work of prose fiction and (drawing partly on the memoirs of voyagers and castaways such as Alexander Selkirk) produced *Robinson Crusoe.* A German critic has called it a "world-book," a label justified not only by the enormous number of translations, imitations, and adaptations that have appeared but by the almost mythic power with which Defoe creates a hero and a situation with which every reader can in some sense identify.

Here (as in his works of the remarkable year 1722, which saw the publication of *Moll Flanders, A Journal of the*

Plague Year, and *Colonel Jack*) Defoe displays his finest gift as a novelist—his insight into human nature. The men and women he writes about are all, it is true, placed in unusual circumstances; they are all, in one sense or another, solitaries; they all struggle, in their different ways, through a life that is a constant scene of jungle warfare; they all become, to some extent, obsessive. They are also ordinary human beings, however, and Defoe, writing always in the first person, enters into their minds and analyzes their motives. His novels are given verisimilitude by their matter-of-fact style and their vivid concreteness of detail; the latter may seem unselective, but it effectively helps to evoke a particular, circumscribed world. Their main defects are shapelessness, an overinsistent moralizing, occasional gaucheness, and naiveté. Defoe's range is narrow, but within that range he is a novelist of considerable power, and his plain, direct style, as in almost all of his writing, holds the reader's interest.

In 1724 he published his last major work of fiction, *Roxana,* though in the closing years of his life, despite failing health, he remained active and enterprising as a writer.

Samuel Richardson

The enthusiasm prompted by Defoe's best novels demonstrated the growing readership for innovative prose narrative. Samuel Richardson, a prosperous London printer, was the next major author to respond to the challenge.

Richardson was 50 years old when he wrote *Pamela*, which was published in 1740, but of his first 50 years little is known. His ancestors were of yeoman stock. His father, also Samuel, and his mother's father, Stephen Hall, became London tradesmen, and his father, after the death of his first wife, married Stephen's daughter, Elizabeth, in 1682.

A temporary move of the Richardsons to Derbyshire accounts for the fact that the novelist was born in Mackworth. They returned to London when Richardson was 10. He had at best what he called "only Common School-Learning." The perceived inadequacy of his education was later to preoccupy him and some of his critics.

Richardson was bound apprentice to a London printer, John Wilde. Sometime after completing his apprenticeship he became associated with the Leakes, a printing family whose presses he eventually took over when he set up in business for himself in 1721 and married Martha Wilde, the daughter of his master. Elizabeth Leake, the sister of a prosperous bookseller of Bath, became his second wife in 1733, two years after Martha's death. His domestic life was marked by tragedy. All six of the children from his first marriage died in infancy or childhood. By his second wife he had four daughters who survived him, but two other children died in infancy. These and other bereavements contributed to the nervous ailments of his later life.

In his professional life Richardson was hardworking and successful. With the growth in prominence of his press went his steady increase in prestige as a member, an officer, and later master, of the Stationers' Company (the guild for those in the book trade). During the 1730s his press became known as one of the three best in London, and with prosperity he moved to a more spacious London house and leased the first of three country houses in which he entertained a circle of friends that included Samuel Johnson, the painter William Hogarth, the actors Colley Cibber and David Garrick, Edward Young, and Arthur Onslow, speaker of the House of Commons, whose influence in 1733 helped to secure for Richardson lucrative contracts for government printing that later included the journals of the House.

Printer turned novelist Samuel Richardson made his mark on the literary scene in 1740, at age 50. The public adored—and some critics deplored—his first novel, Pamela. Hulton Archive/Getty Images

In this same decade Richardson began writing in a modest way. At some point, he was commissioned to write a collection of letters that might serve as models for "country readers," a volume that has become known as *Familiar*

Letters on Important Occasions. Occasionally he hit upon continuing the same subject from one letter to another, and, after a letter from "a father to a daughter in service, on hearing of her master's attempting her virtue," he supplied the daughter's answer. This was the germ of his novel *Pamela.* With a method supplied by the letter writer and a plot by a story that he remembered of an actual serving maid who preserved her virtue and was rewarded by marriage, he began writing the work in November 1739 and published it as *Pamela: or, Virtue Rewarded,* a year later.

Most of the story is told by the heroine herself. On the death of Pamela's mistress, her son, Mr. B, begins a series of stratagems designed to end in Pamela's seduction. These failing, he abducts her and renews his siege in earnest. Pamela preserves her virtue, and halfway through the novel Mr. B offers marriage. In the second half Richardson shows Pamela winning over those who had disapproved of the misalliance. Though the novel was immensely popular, Richardson was criticized by those who thought his heroine a calculating minx or his own morality dubious. Actually his heroine is a vividly imagined blend of the artful and the artless. She is a sadly perplexed girl of 15, with a divided mind, who faces a real dilemma because she wants to preserve her virtue without losing the man with whom she has fallen in love. Since Richardson wrote the novel from Pamela's point of view, it is less clear that Mr. B's problem arises from his having fallen in love with a servant, who, traditionally, would have been merely a target for seduction. In a clever twist, he is converted by her letters, which he has been intercepting and reading. The author resolved the conflicts of both characters too facilely, perhaps, because he was firmly committed to the plot of the true story he had remembered. When the instantaneous popularity of *Pamela* led to a spurious continuation of her story, he wrote his own sequel, *Pamela in her Exalted Condition* (1742), a two-volume work that did little to enhance his reputation.

By 1744 Richardson seems to have completed a first draft of his second novel, *Clarissa: or, The History of a Young Lady,* but he spent three years trying to bring it within the compass of the seven volumes in which it was published, in 1747–48. He first presents the heroine, Clarissa Harlowe, when she is discovering the barely masked motives of her family, who would force her into a loveless marriage to improve their fortunes. Outside the orbit of the Harlowes stands Lovelace, nephew of Lord M and a romantic who held the code of the Harlowes in contempt. In her desperate straits, Clarissa appraises too highly the qualities that set Lovelace beyond the world of her family, and, when he offers protection, she runs off with him. She is physically attracted by if not actually in love with Lovelace and is responsive to the wider horizons of his world, but she is to discover that he wants her only on his own terms.

In Lovelace's letters to his friend Belford, Richardson shows that what is driving him to conquest and finally to rape is really her superiority. In the correspondence of Clarissa and her friend Anna Howe, Richardson shows the distance that separates her from her confidant, who thinks her quixotic in not accepting a marriage; but marriage as a way out would have been a sacrifice to that same consciousness of human dignity that had led her to defy her family. As the novel comes to its long-drawn-out close, she is removed from the world of both the Harlowes and the Lovelaces, and dies, a child of heaven. In providing confidants for his central characters and in refusing to find a place in the social structure into which to fit his sorely beset heroine, Richardson made his greatest advances over *Pamela.* He was determined, as his postscript indicates, to write a novel that was also a tragedy.

Like Pamela, *Richardson's second novel,* Clarissa, *was an epistolary novel, told in the form of letters between characters. The work contains a pointedly tragic ending.* Hulton Archive/Getty Images

Richardson's third novel was his bow to requests for the hero as a good man, a counter-attraction to the errant hero of Henry Fielding's *Tom Jones* (1749). Fielding had been among those who thought Pamela a scheming minx, as he had shown in his parody *An Apology for the Life of Mrs.*

Shamela Andrews (1741). In spite of Fielding's critical praise of *Clarissa* and the friendship that later developed between Richardson and Fielding's sister, Sarah, Richardson never forgave the author of what he stigmatized as "that vile Pamphlet Shamela."

In *The History of Sir Charles Grandison* (1753–54), he provides a hero who is a model of benevolence. He faces little that a good heart cannot remedy and extricates himself from the nearest thing to a dilemma that he has to encounter: a "divided love" between an English woman, Harriet Byron, and an Italian, Signora Clementina. He is saved for Harriet by the last-minute refusal of the Roman Catholic Clementina to marry a firmly committed English churchman. The uneasy minds of Clementina and Harriet are explored with some penetration, but Sir Charles faces nothing in his society or within himself that requires much of a struggle. Furthermore, his dilemma is not so central to the novel as were those of Pamela and Clarissa. He is surrounded with a large cast of characters who have their parts to play in social comedy that anticipates the novel of manners of the late 18th century.

Richardson was an indefatigable reviser of his own work, and the various editions of his novels differ greatly. Much of his revision was undertaken in anxious, self-censoring response to criticism; the earliest versions of his novels are generally the freshest and most daring.

Richardson's *Pamela* is often credited with being the first English *novel*. Although the validity of this claim depends on the definition of the term novel, it is not disputed that Richardson was innovative in his concentration on a single action, in this case a courtship. By telling the story in the form of letters, he provided if not the "stream" at least the flow of consciousness of his characters, and he pioneered in showing how his characters' sense of class differences and their awareness of the conflict between sexual instincts and the moral code created dilemmas that could not always be resolved. These characteristics reappear regularly in the subsequent history of the novel. Above all, Richardson was the writer who made the novel a respectable genre.

Richardson had disciples when he died. Some of them show the influence of *Clarissa,* which seems to have been most responsible for the cult of Richardson that arose on the European continent. It was *Grandison,* however, that set the tone of most of Richardson's English followers and for Jane Austen, who was said to have remembered "every circumstance" in this novel, everything "that was ever said or done." By the end of the 18th century, Richardson's reputation was on the wane both in England and abroad. It was reborn in the late 20th century, however, and *Clarissa* is now widely admired as one of the great psychological novels of European literature.

Epistolary Novel

An epistolary novel is a novel told through the medium of letters written by one or more of the characters. Originating with Samuel Richardson's *Pamela; or, Virtue Rewarded,* it was one of the earliest forms of novel to be developed and remained one of the most popular up to the 19th century. The epistolary novel's reliance on subjective points of view makes it the forerunner of the modern psychological novel.

The advantages of the novel in letter form are that it presents an intimate view of the character's thoughts and feelings without interference from the author and that it conveys the shape of events to come with dramatic immediacy. Also, the presentation of events from several points of view lends the story dimension and verisimilitude. Though the method was most often a vehicle for sentimental novels, it was not limited to them. Of the outstanding examples of the form, Richardson's *Clarissa* (1748) has tragic intensity, Tobias Smollett's *Humphry Clinker* (1771) is a picaresque comedy and social commentary, and Fanny Burney's *Evelina* (1778) is a novel of manners. Jean-Jacques Rousseau used the form as a vehicle for his ideas on marriage and education in *La Nouvelle Héloïse* (1761; "The New Eloise"), and J.W. von Goethe used it for his statement of Romantic despair, *Die Leiden des jungen Werthers* (1774; *The Sorrows of Young Werther*). The letter novel of Pierre Choderlos de Laclos, *Les Liaisons dangereuses* (1782; *Dangerous Acquaintances*), is a work of penetrating and realistic psychology.

Some disadvantages of the form were apparent from the outset. Dependent on the letter writer's need to "confess" to virtue, vice, or powerlessness, such confessions were susceptible to suspicion or ridicule. The servant girl Pamela's remarkable literary powers and her propensity for writing on all occasions were cruelly burlesqued in Henry Fielding's *Shamela* (1741), which pictures his heroine in bed scribbling, "I hear him coming in at the Door," as her seducer enters the room. From 1800 on, the popularity of the form declined, though novels combining letters with journals and narrative were still common. In the 20th century letter fiction was often used to exploit the linguistic humour and unintentional character revelations of such semiliterates as the hero of Ring Lardner's *You Know Me Al* (1916).

Henry Fielding

Henry Fielding turned to novel writing after a successful period as a dramatist, during which his most popular work had been in burlesque forms. Sir Robert Walpole's Licensing Act of 1737, introduced to restrict political satire on the stage, pushed Fielding to look to other genres. He also turned to journalism, of which he wrote a great deal, much of it political. His entry into prose fiction had something in common with the burlesque mode of much of his drama.

As a barrister, Fielding, who rode the Western Circuit (a judicial subdivision of England) twice a year, had little success. In 1740, however, Richardson published his novel *Pamela: or, Virtue Rewarded,* which tells how a servant girl so impressed her master by resistance to his every effort at seduction that in the end "he thought fit to make her his wife." Something new in literature, its success was unparalleled. A crop of imitations followed. In April 1741 there appeared a parody entitled *An Apology for the Life of Mrs. Shamela Andrews,* satirizing Richardson's sentimentality and prudish morality. It was published anonymously and, though Fielding never claimed it, *Shamela* was generally accepted as his work in his lifetime, and stylistic evidence supports the attribution.

Fielding's *Joseph Andrews* was published anonymously in 1742. Described on the title page as "Written in Imitation of the Manner of Cervantes, author of *Don Quixote*," it begins as a burlesque of *Pamela,* with Joseph, Pamela's virtuous footman brother, resisting the attempts of a highborn lady to seduce him. The parodic intention soon becomes secondary, and the novel develops into a masterpiece of sustained irony and social criticism, with, at its centre, Parson Adams, one of the great comic figures of literature and a striking confirmation of the contention of the 19th-century Russian novelist Fyodor Dostoyevsky that the positively good man can be made convincing in fiction only if rendered to some extent ridiculous. Fielding explains in his preface that he is writing "a comic Epic-Poem in Prose." He was certainly inaugurating a new genre in fiction.

Joseph Andrews was written in the most unpropitious circumstances. Fielding was crippled with gout, his six-year-old daughter was dying, and his wife was "in a condition very little better." He was also in financial trouble, from which he was at least temporarily rescued by the generosity of his friend the philanthropist Ralph Allen, who appears in *Tom Jones* as Mr. Allworthy.

In 1743 Fielding published three volumes of *Miscellanies,* works old and new, of which by far the most important is *The Life of Mr. Jonathan Wild the Great.* Here, narrating the life of a notorious criminal of the day, Fielding satirizes human greatness, or rather human greatness confused with power over others. Permanently topical, *Jonathan Wild,* with the exception of some passages by his older contemporary, the Anglo-Irish satirist Jonathan Swift, is perhaps the grimmest satire in English and an exercise in unremitting irony.

After the *Miscellanies* Fielding gave up writing for more than two years, partly, perhaps, out of disappointment with the rewards of authorship, partly in order to devote himself to law.

The History of Tom Jones, a Foundling was published on Feb. 28, 1749. With its great comic gusto, vast gallery of

A lithograph from the pages of Henry Fielding's The History of Tom Jones. *Fielding's comic tale of love overcoming all obstacles helped popularize the novel as a form of entertainment.* Private Collection/The Bridgeman Art Library

characters, and contrasted scenes of high and low life in London and the provinces, it has always constituted the most popular of his works. Like its predecessor, *Joseph Andrews,* it is constructed around a romance plot. The hero, whose true identity remains unknown until the denouement, loves the beautiful Sophia Western, and at the end of the book he wins her hand. Numerous obstacles have to be overcome before he achieves this, however, and in the course of the action the various sets of characters pursue each other from one part of the country to another, giving Fielding an opportunity to paint an incomparably vivid picture of England in the mid-18th century.

The introductory chapters at the beginning of each book make it clear how carefully Fielding had considered the problem of planning the novel. No novelist up until then had so clear an idea of what a novel should be, so that it is not surprising that *Tom Jones* is a masterpiece of literary engineering. The characters fall into several distinct groups—romance characters, villainous characters, Jonsonian "humours," "low" comic characters, and the virtuous Squire Allworthy, who remains in the background and emerges to ensure the conventional happy ending. The novel is further marked by deft alternations between humour and romance, occasional tricks straight from the theatre, and above all the speed and ease of the dialogue. The reading of this work is essential both for an understanding of 18th-century England and for its revelation of the generosity and charity of Fielding's view of humanity.

Two years later *Amelia* was published. Being a much more sombre work, it has always been less popular than *Tom Jones* and *Joseph Andrews.* Fielding's mind must have been darkened by his experiences as a magistrate, as it certainly had been by his wife's death, and *Amelia* is no attempt at the comic epic poem in prose. Rather, it anticipates the Victorian domestic novel, being a study of the relationship between a man and his wife and, in the character of Amelia, a celebration of womanly virtues. It is also Fielding's most intransigent representation of the evils of the society in which he lived, and he clearly finds the spectacle no longer comic.

By 1752, Fielding's gout was so bad that his legs were swathed in bandages, and he often had to use crutches or a wheelchair. In August of 1753 he decided to go to Bath for rest and the waters. That year was a particularly bad one for crime in London, however, and on the eve of his leaving he was invited by Thomas Pelham-Holles, Duke of Newcastle (then secretary of war), to prepare a plan for the Privy Council for the suppression of "those murders and robberies which were every day committed in the streets." His plan, undertaking "to demolish the then reigning gangs" and to establish means of preventing their recurrence, was accepted, and despite the state of his health—to gout had been added asthma and dropsy—he stayed in London for the rest of the year, waging war against criminal gangs with such success that "there was, in the remaining month of November, and in all December, not only no such thing as a murder, but not even a street-robbery committed."

In the following June, Fielding set out for Portugal to seek the sun, writing an account of his journey, *The Journal of a Voyage to Lisbon.* This work presents an extraordinarily vivid picture of the tortuous slowness of 18th-century sea travel, the horrors of contemporary medicine, the caprices of arbitrary power as seen in the conduct of customs officers and other petty officials, and, above all, his indomitable courage and cheerfulness when almost completely helpless, for he could scarcely walk and had to be carried on and off ship. Fielding landed at Lisbon on Aug. 7, 1754. He died in October and was buried in the British cemetery at Lisbon.

Sir Walter Scott called Henry Fielding the "father of the English novel," and the phrase still indicates Fielding's place in the history of literature. Though not actually the first English novelist, he was the first to approach the genre with a fully worked-out theory of the novel; and in *Joseph Andrews, Tom Jones,* and *Amelia,* which a modern critic has called comic epic, epic comedy, and domestic epic, respectively, he had established the tradition of a realism presented in panoramic surveys of contemporary society that dominated English fiction until the end of the 19th century.

Sarah Fielding

(b. Nov. 8, 1710, East Stour, Dorset, Eng.—d. April 9, 1768, Bath, Somerset)

Sarah Fielding was an English author and translator whose novels were among the earliest in the English language and the first to examine the interior lives of women and children.

Fielding was the younger sister of the novelist Henry Fielding, whom many readers believed to be the author of novels she published anonymously, although he denied these speculations in print. She lived with her brother following the death of his wife in 1744. That year she published her first book, *The Adventures of David Simple*, a novel whose comic prose style imitated that of both her brother and his chief literary rival, Samuel Richardson, who was also one of her close friends. With the sequel, *The Adventures of David Simple, Volume the Last: In Which His History Is Concluded* (1753), she developed a style more distinctly her own, which shows greater intricacy of feeling, fuller development of character, and a reduced reliance on plot.

The Governess (1749) is didactic and portrays with comic sensibility the hazards of British social life for the moral development of women. Considered the first novel for girls in the English language, it was an immediate success and went through five editions in Fielding's lifetime while inspiring numerous imitations.

She published only one book under her own name, a translation from the ancient Greek of *Xenophon's Memoirs of Socrates* (1762), a significant achievement in that few women of Fielding's time acquired a scholarly command of Classical languages. Other works include a collaboration with her friend Jane Collier titled *The Cry: A New Dramatic Fable* (1754). Although didacticism frequently overshadows the narrative drive of Fielding's prose, critics credit her as an innovator with a shrewd sense of human motive and keen ironic humour.

Tobias Smollett

Tobias Smollett had no desire to rival Fielding as a formal innovator, and today he seems the less audacious innovator. His novels consequently tend to be rather ragged assemblings of disparate incidents. But, although uneven in performance, all of them include extended passages of real force and idiosyncrasy. His freest writing is expended on grotesque portraiture in which the human is reduced to fiercely energetic automatism. Smollett can also be a stunning reporter of the contemporary scene, whether the subject be a naval battle or the gathering of the decrepit at a spa. His touch is least happy when, complying too facilely with the gathering cult of sensibility, he indulges in rote-learned displays of emotionalism and good-heartedness.

Born in Scotland in 1721, Smollett came of a family of lawyers and soldiers, Whig in politics and Presbyterian in religion. In 1727 or 1728 he entered Dumbarton grammar school, proceeding from there to the University of Glasgow and apprenticeship to William Stirling and John Gordon, surgeons of that city. His first biographer states that he "attended the anatomical and medical lectures," and, if his first novel, *Roderick Random,* may be taken as evidence, he also studied Greek, mathematics, moral and natural philosophy, logic, and belles lettres. He left the university in 1739 without a degree and went to London, taking with him his play *The Regicide.* A year later he was commissioned surgeon's second mate in the Royal Navy and appointed to HMS *Chichester,* which reached Port Royal, Jam., on Jan. 10, 1741. It is probable that Smollett saw action in the naval bombardment of Cartagena (now in Colombia). The expedition was disastrous; he would later describe its horrors in *Roderick Random*. In Jamaica he met and was betrothed to—and perhaps there married—an heiress, Anne Lassells. He returned to London alone to set up as a surgeon on Downing Street, Westminster, his wife joining him in 1747. He failed to secure a production of *The Regicide,* but in 1746, after the defeat of the Jacobite rebels at Culloden, he wrote his most famous poem, "The Tears of Scotland." He had by now moved to cheaper accommodations in Chapel Street, Mayfair, no doubt because, despite litigation, he had managed to recover only a fraction of his wife's considerable dowry, which was invested in land and slaves. It was in Chapel Street that he wrote *Advice* and *Reproof,* verse satires in the manner of the Roman poet Juvenal.

In 1748 Smollett published his novel *The Adventures of Roderick Random,* in part a graphic account of British naval life at the time, and also translated the great picaresque romance *Gil Blas* from the French of Alain-René Lesage. In 1750 he obtained the degree of M.D. from Marischal College, Aberdeen. Later in the year he was in Paris, searching out material for *The Adventures of Peregrine Pickle*. This work contains a great comic figure in Hawser Trunnion, a retired naval officer who, though living on dry land, insists on behaving as though he were still on the quarterdeck of one of his majesty's ships at sea.

In 1752 he published "An Essay on the External Use of Water," an attack on the medicinal properties of the waters of a popular English health resort, Bath (he would resume the attack in his later novel *The Expedition of Humphry Clinker*). The essay made him many enemies and little money. His financial difficulties were intensified by his generosity in lending money to a hack writer called Peter Gordon, who employed legal stratagems to avoid repayment. Smollett came to blows with Gordon and his landlord and was sued by them for £1,000 and £500, respectively, on charges of trespass and assault. In the event, Smollett was required to pay only small damages. He was now living at Monmouth House, Chelsea, where he was host to such leading literary figures as the authors Samuel Johnson and Oliver Goldsmith, as well as to the actor David Garrick and John Hunter, a famous surgeon and anatomist. On Sundays, if one may take a passage in *Peregrine Pickle* as autobiographical, Smollett threw his house open to "unfortunate brothers of the quill," whom he regaled with "beer, pudding, and potatoes, port, punch, and Calvert's entire butt-beer." He himself seems to have been a man irascible, pugnacious, infinitely energetic, courageous, and generous.

The Adventures of Ferdinand, Count Fathom (now, with *The History and Adventures of an Atom,* the least regarded of his novels) appeared in 1753. It sold poorly, and Smollett was forced into borrowing from friends and into further hack writing. In June 1753 he visited Scotland for the first time in 15 years; his mother, it is said, recognized him only because of his "roguish smile." Back in London, Smollett set about a commitment to translate *Don Quixote* from the Spanish of Miguel de Cervantes, and this translation was published in 1755. Smollett was already suffering from tuberculosis. Early in 1756 he became editor of *The Critical Review,* a Tory and church paper, at the same time writing his *Complete History of England,* which was financially successful. This work relieved the financial pressure that he had felt all his adult life. A year later, his farce *The Reprisal: or, The Tars of Old England* was produced at Drury Lane and brought him a profit of almost £200. In 1758 he became what today might perhaps be called general editor of *Universal History,* a compilation of 58 volumes; Smollett himself wrote on France, Italy, and Germany. His friendship with the politician John Wilkes enabled him to secure the release of Francis Barber, Samuel Johnson's black servant, from the press-gang. But a libel on Admiral Sir Charles Knowles in *The Critical Review* led to Smollett's being sentenced to a fine of £100 and three months' imprisonment in the King's Bench Prison. He seems to have lived there in some comfort and drew on his experiences for his novel *The Adventures of Sir Launcelot Greaves* (1762), which was serialized in *The British Magazine,* of which Smollett became editor in 1760.

Two years later he became editor of *The Briton,* a weekly founded to support the prime minister John Stuart, 3rd Earl of Bute. He was also writing an eight-volume work entitled *The Present State of all Nations,* and he had begun a translation, in 36 volumes, of the varied works of the French writer Voltaire. Smollett was now seriously ill; attempts to secure a post as physician to the army in Portugal and as British consul in Marseille or Madrid were fruitless. In 1763 the death of his only child, Elizabeth, who was 15 years old, overwhelmed him "with unutterable sorrow." He severed his connection with *The Critical Review* and, as he said, "every other literary system," retiring with his wife to France, where he settled at Nice.

In 1766 Smollett published *Travels Through France and Italy,* his one nonfiction work that is still read. It is a satire on both tourists and those who batten on them, and its jaundiced version of traveling on the Continent led to Smollett's appearance as the splenetic Smelfungus in Laurence Sterne's novel *A Sentimental Journey* (1768). He returned to England in that year, visited Scotland, and at Christmas was again in England (at Bath), where he probably began what is his finest work, *The Expedition of Humphry Clinker,* an epistolary novel that recounts the adventures of a family traveling through Britain. In 1768, steadily weakening in health, he retired to Pisa, Italy. During the autumn of 1770 he seems to have written the bulk of *Humphry Clinker,* which was published on June 15, 1771. He died three months later.

Smollett is not the equal of his older contemporaries, the novelists Samuel Richardson and Henry Fielding, but he is unrivaled for the pace and vigour that sustain his comedy. He is especially brilliant in the rendering of comic characters in their externals, thus harking back to the manner of the Jacobean playwright Ben Jonson and looking forward to that of the novelist Charles Dickens. By modern criteria, his art as a satirical novelist is defective, his model being the "picaresque" novel, relating loosely linked episodes in the life of a rogue hero. But his panoramic picture of the life of his times is surpassed only by that given by Henry Fielding, while his account of conditions in the Royal Navy is especially valuable.

Picaresque Novel

A picaresque novel, usually a first-person narrative, relates the adventures of a rogue or low-born adventurer (Spanish *pícaro*) as he (or, less often, she) drifts from place to place and from one social milieu to another in his effort to survive. In its episodic structure the picaresque novel resembles the long, rambling romances of medieval chivalry, to which it provided the first realistic counterpart. Unlike the idealistic knight-errant hero, however, the picaro is a cynical and amoral rascal who, if given half a chance, would rather live by his wits than by honourable work. The picaro wanders about and has adventures among people from all social classes and professions, often just barely escaping punishment for his own lying, cheating, and stealing. He is a casteless outsider who feels inwardly unrestrained by prevailing social codes and mores, and he conforms outwardly to them only when it serves his own ends. The picaro's narrative becomes in effect an ironic or satirical survey of the hypocrisies and corruptions of society, while also offering the reader a rich mine of observations concerning people in low or humble walks of life.

The picaresque novel originated in Spain with *Lazarillo de Tormes* (1554; doubtfully attributed to Diego Hurtado de Mendoza), in which the poor boy Lazaro describes his services under seven successive lay and clerical masters, each of whose dubious character is hidden under a mask of hypocrisy. The irreverent wit of *Lazarillo* helped make it one of the most widely read books of its time. The next picaresque novel to be published, Mateo Alemán's *Guzmán de Alfarache* (1599), became the true prototype of the genre and helped establish realism as the dominant trend in the Spanish novel. The supposed autobiography of the son of a ruined Genoese moneylender, this work is richer in invention, variety of episode, and presentation of character than *Lazarillo,* and it too enjoyed extraordinary popularity.

Among *Guzmán*'s numerous successors were several short novels by Miguel de Cervantes in the picaresque manner, notably *Rinconete y Cortadillo* (1613) and *El Coloquio de los perros* (1613; "Colloquy of the Dogs"). Francisco López de Úbeda's *La picara Justina* (1605; "Naughty Justina") tells the story of a woman picaro who deceives her lovers just as the picaro does his masters. Francisco Gómez de Quevedo's *Vida del Buscón* (1626; "The Life of a Scoundrel") is a masterpiece of the genre, in which the profound psychological depiction of a petty thief and swindler is underlain by a deep concern for moral values. After *Buscón* the picaresque novel in Spain declined gradually into the novel of adventure.

In the meantime, however, the picaro had made his way into other European literatures after *Lazarillo de Tormes* was translated into French, Dutch, and English in the later 16th century. The first picaresque novel in England was Thomas Nashe's *Unfortunate Traveller, or, the Life of Jacke Wilton* (1594). In Germany the type was represented by H.J. von Grimmelshausen's *Simplicissimus* (1669). In England the female picaro was revived in Daniel Defoe's *Moll Flanders* (1722), and many picaresque elements can be found in Henry Fielding's *Jonathan Wild* (1725), *Joseph Andrews* (1742), and *Tom Jones* (1749), and Tobias Smollett's *Roderick Random* (1748), *Peregrine Pickle* (1751), and *Ferdinand, Count Fathom* (1753). The outstanding French example is Alain René Lesage's *Gil Blas* (1715–35), which preserves a Spanish setting and borrows incidents from forgotten Spanish novels but portrays a gentler, more humanized picaro.

In the mid-18th century the growth of the realistic novel with its tighter, more elaborated plot and its greater development of character led to the final decline of the picaresque novel, which came to be considered somewhat inferior in artistry. But the opportunities for satire provided by the picaresque novel's mingling of characters from all walks of life, its vivid descriptions of industries and professions, its realistic language and detail, and above all its ironic and detached survey of manners and morals helped to enrich the realistic novel and contributed to that form's development in the 18th and 19th centuries. Elements of the picaresque novel proper reappeared in such mature realistic novels as Nikolay Gogol's *Dead Souls* (1842–52), Mark Twain's *Huckleberry Finn* (1884), and Thomas Mann's *Confessions of Felix Krull* (1954).

Laurence Sterne

An experiment of a radical and seminal kind is Laurence Sterne's *Tristram Shandy* (1759–67), which, drawing on a tradition of learned wit from Erasmus and Rabelais to Burton and Swift, provides a brilliant comic critique of the progress of the English novel through the middle of the 18th century.

Sterne's father, Roger, though grandson of an archbishop of York, was an infantry officer of the lowest rank who fought in many battles during the War of the Spanish Succession (1701–14). In Flanders, Roger married Agnes, the widow of an officer, but of a social class much below Roger's. The regiment retired to Ireland, and there Laurence was born, in 1713. Most of his early childhood was spent in poverty, following the troops about Ireland. Later, Sterne expressed his affection for soldiers through his portraits in *Tristram Shandy* of the gentle uncle Toby and Corporal Trim.

At age 10, Sterne was sent to school at Hipperholme, near Halifax, where his uncle, Richard Sterne, whose estate was nearby, could look out for him. He grew into a tall, thin man, with a long nose but likable face. Sterne attended Jesus College, Cambridge, on a scholarship. At college he met his great friend John Hall-Stevenson (Eugenius in his fiction) and also suffered his first severe hemorrhage of the lungs. He had incurable tuberculosis.

After graduating he took holy orders and became vicar of Sutton-on-the-Forest, north of York. He soon became a prebendary (or canon) of York Minster and acquired the vicarage of Stillington. At first he was helped by another uncle, Jaques Sterne, precentor of York and archdeacon of Cleveland, a powerful clergyman but a mean-tempered man and a rabid politician. In 1741–42 Sterne wrote political articles supporting the administration of Sir Robert Walpole for a newspaper founded by his uncle but soon withdrew from politics in disgust. His uncle became his archenemy, thwarting his advancement whenever possible.

Sterne fell in love with Elizabeth Lumley, a cousin to Elizabeth Montagu, the bluestocking. They married in

1741. According to the account of an acquaintance, Sterne's infidelities were a cause of discord in the marriage.

As a clergyman Sterne worked hard but erratically. In two ecclesiastical courts he served as commissary (judge), and his frequent sermons at York Minster were popular. Externally, his life was typical of the moderately successful clergy. But Elizabeth, who had several stillborn children, was unhappy. Only one child, Lydia, lived.

In 1759, to support his dean in a church squabble, Sterne wrote *A Political Romance* (later called *The History of a Good Warm Watch-Coat*), a Swiftian satire of dignitaries of the spiritual courts. At the demands of embarrassed churchmen, the book was burned. Thus, Sterne lost his chances for clerical advancement but discovered his real talents. Turning over his parishes to a curate, he began *Tristram Shandy*. An initial, sharply satiric version was rejected by Robert Dodsley, the London printer, just when Sterne's personal life was upset. His mother and uncle both died. His wife had a nervous breakdown and threatened suicide. Sterne continued his comic novel, but every sentence, he said, was "written under the greatest heaviness of heart." In this mood, he softened the satire and told about Tristram's opinions, his eccentric family, and ill-fated childhood with a sympathetic humour, sometimes hilarious, sometimes sweetly melancholic—a comedy skirting tragedy.

At his own expense, Sterne published the first two volumes of *The Life and Opinions of Tristram Shandy, Gentleman* at York late in 1759, but he sent half of the imprint to Dodsley to sell in London. By March 1760, when he went to London, *Tristram Shandy* was the rage, and he was famous. Dodsley's brother James, the new proprietor, brought out a second edition of the novel, and two volumes of sermons followed.

The witty, naughty "Tristram Shandy," or "Parson Yorick," as Sterne was called after characters in his novel, was the most sought-after man in town. Although the timing was coincidental, Lord Fauconberg, a Yorkshire neighbour, presented him with a third parish, Coxwold. Sterne returned north joyfully to settle at Coxwold in his beloved "Shandy Hall," a charming old house that is now a museum. He began to write at Shandy Hall during the summers, going to London in the winter to publish what he had written. James Dodsley brought out two more volumes of *Tristram Shandy;* thereafter, Sterne became his own publisher. In London he enjoyed the company of many great people, but his nights were sometimes wild. In 1762, after almost dying from lung hemorrhages, he fled the damp air of England into France, a journey he described as Tristram's flight from death. This and a later trip abroad gave him much material for his later *Sentimental Journey.* Elizabeth, now recovered, followed him to France, where she and their daughter settled permanently. Sterne returned to England virtually a single man.

In 1767 he published the final volume of *Tristram Shandy*. Soon thereafter he fell in love with Eliza Draper, who was half his age and unhappily married to an official of the East India Company. They carried on an open, sentimental flirtation, but Eliza was under a promise to return to her husband in Bombay. After she sailed, Sterne finished *A Sentimental Journey Through France and Italy, by Mr. Yorick,* published it to acclaim early in 1768, and collapsed.

Lying in his London lodgings, he put up his arm as though to ward off a blow, saying, "Now it is come," and died in March 1768. Soon after burial at London, Sterne's body was stolen by grave robbers, taken to Cambridge, and used for an anatomy lecture. Someone recognized the body, and it was quietly returned to the grave. The story, only whispered at the time, was confirmed in 1969: Sterne's remains were exhumed and now rest in the churchyard at Coxwold, close to Shandy Hall.

Sterne's *Tristram Shandy* was published in nine slim volumes (released in five installments) from 1759 to 1767. In it the narrator, Tristram, sets out to do the impossible—to tell the story of his life. He begins with the story of his conception—an innocent remark of his mother upsetting his father's concentration and causing poor Tristram to be conceived a weakling. To understand that, Tristram must then explain John Locke's principle of the association of ideas. This, in turn, embroils him in a discussion of his parents' marriage contract, his Uncle Toby, Parson Yorick, the midwife, and Dr. Slop. He has so much to tell that he does not get himself born until the third volume. Finally reality dawns upon Tristram: it takes more time to tell the story of his life than it does to live it; he can never catch himself.

At one level *Tristram Shandy* is a satire upon intellectual pride. Walter Shandy thinks he can beget and rear the perfect child, yet Tristram is misconceived, misbaptized, miseducated, and circumcised by a falling window sash. He grows to manhood an impotent weakling whose only hope of transcending death is to tell the story of himself and his family. Finally, Tristram turns to the sweet, funny story of his Uncle Toby's amours with the Widow Wadman, concluding the novel at a point in time years before Tristram was born. A hilarious, often ribald novel, *Tristram Shandy* nevertheless makes a serious comment on the isolation of people from each other caused by the inadequacies of language and describes the breaking-through of isolation by impulsive gestures of sympathy and love. A second great theme of the novel is that of time—the discrepancy between clock time and time as sensed, the impinging of the past upon the present, the awareness that a joyous life inexorably leads to death. Modern commentators regard *Tristram Shandy* as the ancestor of psychological and stream-of-consciousness fiction.

Sentimental Novel

A sentimental novel is, broadly, any novel that exploits the reader's capacity for tenderness, compassion, or sympathy to a disproportionate degree by presenting a beclouded or unrealistic view of its subject. In a restricted sense the term refers to a widespread European novelistic development of the 18th century, which arose partly in reaction to the austerity and rationalism of the Neoclassical period. The sentimental novel exalted feeling above reason and raised the analysis of emotion to a fine art. An early example in France is Antoine-François Prévost's *Manon Lescaut* (1731), the story of a courtesan for whom a young seminary student of noble birth forsakes his career, family, and religion and ends as a card shark and confidence man. His downward progress, if not actually excused, is portrayed as a sacrifice to love.

The assumptions underlying the sentimental novel were Jean-Jacques Rousseau's doctrine of the natural goodness of man and his belief that moral development was fostered by experiencing powerful sympathies. In England, Samuel Richardson's sentimental novel *Pamela* (1740) was recommended by clergymen as a means of educating the heart. In the 1760s the sentimental novel developed into the "novel of sensibility," which presented characters possessing a pronounced susceptibility to delicate sensation. Such characters were not only deeply moved by sympathy for their fellow man but also reacted emotionally to the beauty inherent in natural settings and works of art and music. The prototype was Laurence Sterne's *Tristram Shandy* (1759–67), which devotes several pages to describing Uncle Toby's horror of killing a fly. The literature of Romanticism adopted many elements of the novel of sensibility, including responsiveness to nature and belief in the wisdom of the heart and in the power of sympathy. It did not, however, assimilate the novel of sensibility's characteristic optimism.

Sterne's second and last novel, *A Sentimental Journey,* is the story of Yorick's travels through France; Sterne did not live to complete the part on Italy. He called it a "sentimental" journey because the point of travel was not to see sights or visit art collections, but to make meaningful contact with people. Yorick succeeds, but in every adventure, his ego or inappropriate desires and impulses get in the way of "sentimental commerce." The result is a lighthearted comedy of moral sentiments. *A Sentimental Journey* was translated into many languages, but the translations tended to lose the comedy and emphasize the sentiments. Abroad Sterne became the "high priest of sentimentalism," and as such had a profound impact upon continental letters in the second half of the 18th century.

Fanny Burney

Among the most engaging and thoughtful lesser-known novelists of the period is Fanny Burney, who was also an evocative and self-revelatory diarist and letter writer. The daughter of the musician Charles Burney, she wrote *Evelina*, a landmark in the development of the novel of manners.

Born in 1752, Burney educated herself by omnivorous reading at home. Her literary apprenticeship was much influenced by her father's friend Samuel Crisp, a disappointed author living in retirement. It was to "Daddy" Crisp that she addressed her first journal letters, lively accounts of the musical evenings at the Burneys' London house where the elite among European performers entertained informally for gatherings that might include David Garrick, Samuel Johnson, Edmund Burke, and Richard Sheridan. Considered the least promising of the Burney children, she moved unnoticed in the circles of the great, confiding her observations to Crisp.

Portrait of Fanny Burney, whose diary entries sparked the creation of her first novel, Evelina. *Burney popularized the novel of manners, a literary form that Jane Austen would later master.* Rischgitz/Hulton Archive/Getty Image

Her practice of observing and recording society led eventually to her novel *Evelina, or The History of a Young Lady's Entrance into the World*. *Evelina* revealed its author to be a keen social commentator with an attentive ear for dialect and the differentiation of London speech.

It concerns the development of a young girl, unsure of herself in society and subject to errors of manners and judgment. The plot terminates with Evelina's marriage after the mistakes stemming from her untutored girlhood have been surmounted. A novel treating contemporary manners in an elegant and decorous way and depending for the development of its plot upon the erring and uncertain conduct of the heroine was an innovation that pointed the way for the novels of Jane Austen. Published anonymously in 1778, *Evelina* took London by storm.

When the secret of Burney's authorship was revealed, her debut into literary society was launched by the fashionable hostess Hester Thrale. Once the young woman overcame her shyness she could match wits with Johnson himself, who showed his kindness to her between 1779 and 1783 when they both made long visits to the Thrales. Burney's journals from this period have been prized for their vignettes of contemporary scenes and celebrities and for Burney's own secretly expressed delight in being famous.

Her next novel, *Cecilia, or Memoirs of an Heiress*, 5 vol. (1782), incorporated morally didactic themes along with the social satire of Burney's first novel into a more complex plot. Though lacking the freshness and spontaneity of *Evelina*, this novel was equally well received, but Burney's success was shadowed by the death of Henry Thrale in 1781, of Crisp in 1783, and of Johnson in 1784. These years also brought a disappointment in love, when the ambiguous attentions of a young clergyman came to nothing.

In 1785 Burney was presented to Queen Charlotte and King George III and in 1786 was invited to court as second keeper of the robes, where she remained for five unhappy years. Eventually her health suffered, and she was allowed to resign in 1791. Her journals of the period loyally repress court gossip of the years of the king's madness (1788–89) but contain accounts of public events like the trial of Warren Hastings.

In 1793, when she was 41, Burney married Alexandre d'Arblay, a former adjutant general to Lafayette, then a penniless French émigré living in England. They had one son. In 1796 she wrote a potboiler, *Camilla: or a Picture of Youth*, and on its proceeds the d'Arblays built a house in Surrey, where they moved in 1797. While on a visit to France with her husband and son in 1802, she was forced by the renewal of the Napoleonic Wars to stay for 10 years. After Waterloo (1815) the d'Arblays returned and settled at Bath, where d'Arblay died in 1818. Mme d'Arblay then retired to London, where she devoted her attention to her son's career and to the publication of her father's *Memoirs* (1832). She died in 1840.

POETS AND POETRY AFTER POPE

Eighteenth-century poetry after Pope produced nothing that can compete with achievements on the scale of *Clarissa* and *Tristram Shandy*, but much that was vital was accomplished. William Collins's *Odes on Several Descriptive and Allegoric Subjects* (1747), for instance, displays great technical ingenuity and a resonant insistence on the imagination and the passions as poetry's true realm. The odes also mine vigorously the potentiality of personification as a medium for poetic expression. In *An Elegy Written in a Country Church Yard* (1751), Thomas Gray revisited the terrain of such recent poems as Thomas Parnell's *Night-Piece on Death* (1722) and Robert Blair's *The Grave* (1743) and discovered a tensely humane eloquence far beyond his predecessors' powers. In later odes, particularly *The Progress of Poesy* (1757), Gray successfully sought close imitation of the original Pindaric form, even emulating Greek rhythms in English, while developing ambitious ideas about cultural continuity and renewal. Gray's fascination with the potency of primitive art (as evidenced in another great ode, *The Bard*, 1757) is part of a larger movement of taste, of which the contemporary enthusiasm for James Macpherson's alleged translations of *Ossian* (1760–63) is a further indicator.

Another eclectically learned and energetically experimental poet is Christopher Smart, whose renown rests largely on two poems. *Jubilate Agno* (written during confinement in various asylums between 1758/59 and 1763 but not published until 1939) is composed in free verse and experiments with applying the antiphonal principles of Hebrew poetry to English. *A Song to David* (1763) is a rhapsodic hymn of praise, blending enormous linguistic vitality with elaborate structural patterning. Both contain encyclopaedic gatherings of recondite and occult lore, numerous passages of which modern scholarship has yet to explicate satisfactorily, but the poetry is continually energized by minute alterations of tone, startling conjunctions of material, and a unique alertness to the mystery of the commonplace.

Smart was also a superb writer of hymns, a talent in which his major contemporary rival was William Cowper in his *Olney Hymns* (1779). Both are worthy successors to the richly inventive work of Isaac Watts in the first half of the century. Elsewhere, Cowper can write with buoyant humour and satiric relaxation, as when, for instance, he wryly observes from the safety of rural seclusion the evils of town life. But some of his most characterful poetry emerges from a painfully intense experience of withdrawal and isolation. His rooted Calvinism caused him periods of acute despair when he could see no hope of admission to salvation, a mood chronicled with grim precision in his masterly short poem *The Castaway* (written 1799). His most extended achievement is *The Task* (1785), an extraordinary fusion of disparate interests, working calmly toward religious praise and pious acceptance.

There was also a significant number of inventive and sometimes popular women poets in the period. "Literary ladies" were often celebrated and sometimes became respected public figures. Their poetic ventures were encouraged by the growth in publishing generally and, in particular, by the invention of magazines and literary journals. Many of the leading women poets of the period first published in *Gentleman's Magazine*. The most notable woman poet of the early 18th century is probably Lady Mary Montagu, who still composed for manuscript circulation rather than publication. She also wrote, in letters, her sparkling *Embassy to Constantinople* (often called *Turkish Letters*), published posthumously in 1763. Notable female poets later in the century include Mary Leapor, a Northhamptonshire kitchen servant who was also a witty verse satirist, celebrated by contemporaries only after her early death. Much admired in their own lifetimes were Anna Seward and Hannah More, both of whom wrote much miscellaneous prose as well as poetry, and Charlotte Smith, whose sonnets were hugely popular in the 1780s.

Robert Burns

The 1780s brought publishing success to Robert Burns for his *Poems, Chiefly in the Scottish Dialect* (1786). Drawing on the precedents of Allan Ramsay and Robert Fergusson, Burns demonstrated how Scottish idioms and ballad modes could lend a new vitality to the language of poetry. His work bears the imprint of the revolutionary decades in which he wrote, and recurrent in much of it are a joyful hymning of freedom, both individual and national, and an instinctive belief in the possibility of a new social order.

Life

Burns's father had come to Ayrshire from Kincardineshire in an endeavour to improve his fortunes, but, though he worked immensely hard first on the farm of Mount Oliphant, which he leased in 1766, and then on that of Lochlea, which he took in 1777, till luck dogged him, and he died in 1784, worn out and bankrupt. It was watching his father being thus beaten down that helped to make Robert, who was born in 1759, both a rebel against the social order of his day and a bitter satirist of all forms of religious and political thought that condoned or perpetuated inhumanity. He received some formal schooling from a teacher as well as sporadically from other sources. He acquired a superficial reading knowledge of French and a bare smattering of Latin, and he read most of the important 18th-century English writers as well as Shakespeare, Milton, and Dryden. His knowledge of Scottish literature was confined in his childhood to orally transmitted folk songs and folk tales together with a modernization of the late 15th-century poem "Wallace." His religion throughout his adult life seems to have been a humanitarian deism.

Proud, restless, and full of a nameless ambition, the young Burns did his share of hard work on the farm. His father's death made him tenant of the farm of Mossgiel to which the family moved and freed him to seek male and female companionship where he would. He took sides against the dominant extreme Calvinist wing of the church in Ayrshire and championed a local gentleman, Gavin Hamilton, who had got into trouble with the Kirk Session for sabbath breaking. He had an affair with a servant girl at the farm, Elizabeth Paton, who in 1785 bore his first illegitimate child, and on the child's birth he welcomed it with a lively poem.

Robert Burns's poetry can be considered both nationalistic, for its use of Scots idioms and ballads, and universal, for its recurring theme of individual freedom. Hulton Archive/Getty Images

Burns developed rapidly throughout 1784 and 1785 as an "occasional" poet who more and more turned to verse to express his emotions of love, friendship, or amusement or his ironical contemplation of the social scene. But these were not spontaneous effusions by an almost-illiterate peasant. Burns was a conscious craftsman; his entries in the commonplace book that he had begun in 1783 reveal that from the beginning he was interested in the technical problems of versification.

Though he wrote poetry for his own amusement and that of his friends, Burns remained restless and dissatisfied. He won the reputation of being a dangerous rebel against orthodox religion, and, when in 1786 he fell in love with Jean Armour, her father refused to allow her to marry Burns even though a child was on the way and under Scots law mutual consent followed by consummation constituted a legal marriage. Jean was persuaded by her father to go back on her promise. Robert, hurt and enraged, took up with another girl, Mary Campbell, who died soon after. On September 3, Jean bore him twins out of wedlock.

Meanwhile, the farm was not prospering, and Burns, harassed by insoluble problems, thought of emigrating. But he first wanted to show his country what he could do. In the midst of his troubles he went ahead with his plans for publishing a volume of his poems at the nearby town of Kilmarnock. It was entitled *Poems, Chiefly in the Scottish Dialect* and appeared on July 31, 1786. Its success was immediate and overwhelming. Simple country folk and sophisticated Edinburgh critics alike hailed it, and the upshot was that Burns set out for Edinburgh on Nov. 27, 1786, to be lionized, patronized, and showered with well-meant but dangerous advice.

The Kilmarnock volume was a remarkable mixture. It included a handful of first-rate Scots poems: "The Twa Dogs," "Scotch Drink," "The Holy Fair," "An Address to the Deil," "The Death and Dying Words of Poor Maillie," "To a Mouse," "To a Louse," and some others, including a number of verse letters addressed to various friends. There were also a few Scots poems in which he was unable to sustain his inspiration or that are spoiled by a confused purpose. In addition, there were six gloomy and histrionic poems in English, four songs, of which only one, "It Was Upon a Lammas Night," showed promise of his future greatness as a song writer, and what to contemporary reviewers seemed the stars of the volume, "The Cotter's Saturday Night" and "To a Mountain Daisy."

Burns selected his Kilmarnock poems with care: he was anxious to impress a genteel Edinburgh audience. In his preface he played up to contemporary sentimental views about the natural man and the noble peasant, exaggerated his lack of education, pretended to a lack of natural resources, and in general acted a part. The trouble was that he was only half acting. He was uncertain enough about the genteel tradition to accept much of it at its face value, and though, to his ultimate glory, he kept returning to what his own instincts told him was the true path for him to follow, far too many of his poems are marred by a naïve and sentimental moralizing.

Edinburgh unsettled Burns, and, after a number of amorous and other adventures there and several trips to other parts of Scotland, he settled in the summer of 1788 at a farm in Ellisland, Dumfriesshire. At Edinburgh, too, he arranged for a new and enlarged edition (1787) of his *Poems,* but little of significance was added to the Kilmarnock selection. He found farming at Ellisland difficult, though he was helped by Jean Armour, with whom he had been reconciled and whom he finally married in 1788.

In Edinburgh Burns had met James Johnson, a keen collector of Scottish songs who was bringing out a series of volumes of songs with the music and who enlisted Burns's help in finding, editing, improving, and rewriting items. Burns was enthusiastic and soon became virtual editor of Johnson's *The Scots Musical Museum.* Later, he became involved with a similar project for George Thomson, but Thomson was a more consciously genteel person than Johnson, and Burns had to fight with him to prevent him from "refining" words and music and so ruining their character. Johnson's *The Scots Musical Museum* (1787–1803) and the first five volumes of Thomson's *A Select Collection of Original Scotish Airs for the Voice* (1793–1818) contain the bulk of Burns's songs. Burns spent the latter part of his life in assiduously collecting and writing songs to provide words for traditional Scottish airs. He regarded his work as service to Scotland and quixotically refused payment. The only poem he wrote after his Edinburgh visit that showed a hitherto unsuspected side of his poetic genius was *Tam o'Shanter* (1791), a spirited, narrative poem in brilliantly handled eight-syllable couplets based on a folk legend.

Meanwhile, Burns corresponded with and visited on terms of equality a great variety of literary and other people who were considerably "above" him socially. He was an admirable letter writer and a brilliant talker, and he could hold his own in any company. At the same time, he was still a struggling tenant farmer, and the attempt to keep himself going in two different social and intellectual capacities was wearing him down. After trying for a long time, he finally obtained a post in the excise service in 1789 and moved to Dumfries in 1791, where he lived until his death, in 1796. His life at Dumfries was active. He wrote numerous "occasional" poems and did an immense amount of work for the two song collections, in addition to carrying out his duties as exciseman. The outbreak of the French Revolution excited him, and some indiscreet outbursts nearly lost him his job, but his reputation as a good exciseman and a politic but humiliating recantation saved him.

Influence

Burns was a man of great intellectual energy and force of character who, in a class-ridden society, never found an environment in which he could fully exercise his personality. The fact is that Scottish culture in his day could provide no intellectual background that might replace the Calvinism that Burns rejected. The Edinburgh literati of Burns's day were second raters, but the problem was more than one of personalities. The only substitute for the rejected Calvinism seemed to be a sentimental deism, a facile belief in the good heart as all, and this was not a creed rich or complex enough to nourish great poetry. That Burns in spite of this produced so much fine poetry shows the strength of his unique genius, and that he has become the Scottish national poet is a tribute to his hold on the popular imagination.

Burns perhaps exhibited his greatest poetic powers in his satires. There is also a remarkable craftsmanship in his verse letters, which display a most adroit counterpointing of the colloquial and the formal. But it is by his songs that Burns is best known, and it is his songs that have carried his reputation round the world. Burns is without doubt the greatest songwriter Great Britain has produced.

Burns wrote all his songs to known tunes, sometimes writing several sets of words to the same air in an endeavour to find the most apt poem for a given melody. Many songs which, it is clear from a variety of evidence, must have been substantially written by Burns he never claimed as his. He never claimed "Auld Lang Syne," for example, which he described simply as an old fragment he had discovered, but the song we have is almost certainly his, though the chorus and probably the first stanza are old. (Burns wrote it for a simple and moving old air that is *not* the tune to which it is now sung, as Thomson set it to another tune.) The full extent of Burns's work on Scottish song will probably never be known.

It is positively miraculous that Burns was able to enter into the spirit of older folk song and re-create, out of an old chorus, such songs as "I'm O'er Young to Marry Yet," "Green Grow the Rashes, O," and a host of others. It is this uncanny ability to speak with the great anonymous voice of the Scottish people that explains the special feeling that Burns arouses, feelings that manifest themselves in the "Burns cult."

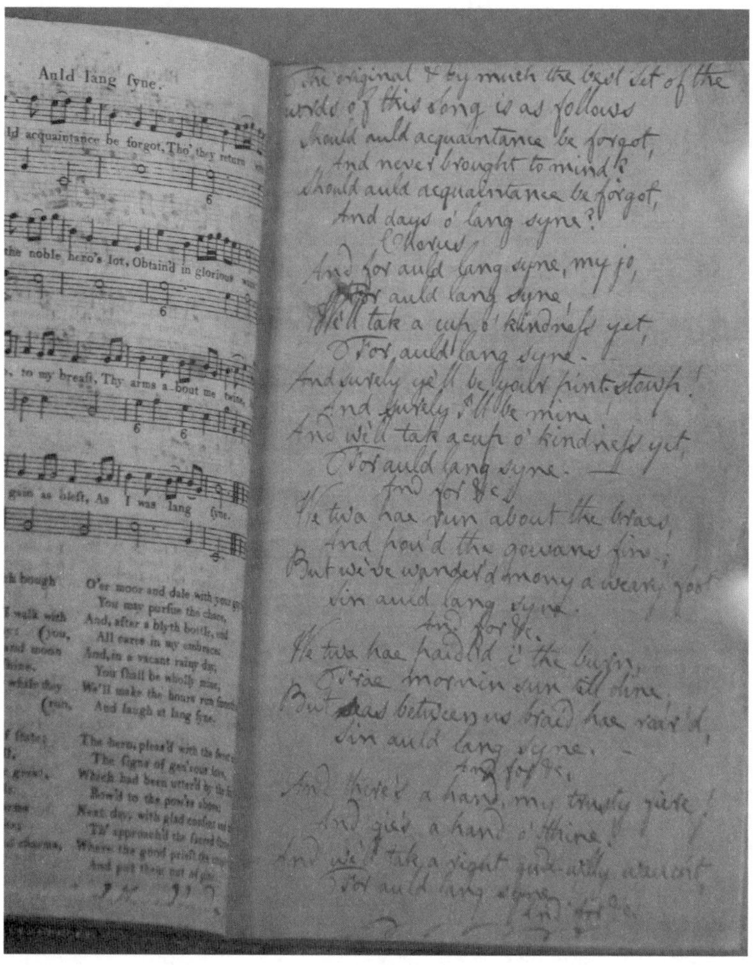

The manuscript and lyrics to Robert Burns's "Auld Lang Syne," as displayed at auction on Aug. 11, 2009, in Edinburgh, Scot. Burns was a gifted lyricist as well as a poet. Jeff J. Mitchell/Getty Images

Oliver Goldsmith

Another major poet who achieved distinction in an impressive array of nondramatic modes is Oliver Goldsmith, whose contemporary fame as a poet rested chiefly on *The Traveller* (1764), *The Deserted Village* (1770), and the incomplete *Retaliation* (1774). The last, published 15 days after his own death, is a dazzling series of character portraits in the form of mock epitaphs on a group of his closest acquaintances. *The Traveller*, a philosophical comparison of the differing national cultures of western Europe and the degrees of happiness their citizens enjoy, is narrated by a restless wanderer whose heart yet yearns after his own native land, where his brother still dwells. In *The Deserted Village* the experience is one of enforced exile, as an idealized village community is ruthlessly broken up in the interests of landed power.

A comparable story of a rural idyll destroyed (though this time narrative artifice allows its eventual restoration) is at the centre of Goldsmith's greatly popular novel, *The Vicar of Wakefield* (1766). He was also a deft and energetic practitioner of the periodical essay, contributing to at least eight journals between 1759 and 1773. His *Citizen of the World*, a series of essays originally published in *The Public Ledger* in 1760–61, uses the device of a Chinese traveler whose letters home comment tolerantly but shrewdly on his English experiences.

Samuel Johnson's Poetry and Prose

Goldsmith belonged to the circle of a writer of still ampler range and outstanding intellect, Samuel Johnson. Pope recognized Johnson's poetic promise as it was exhibited in *London* (1738), an invigorating reworking of Juvenal's third satire as a castigation of the decadence of contemporary Britain. Johnson's finest poem, *The Vanity of Human Wishes* (1749), also takes its cue from Juvenal, this time his 10th satire. It is a tragic meditation on the pitiful spectacle of human unfulfillment, yet it ends with an urgent prayer of Christian hope.

But, great poet though he was, the lion's share of Johnson's formidable energies was expended on prose and on editorial work. From his early years in London, he lived by his pen and gave himself unstintingly to satisfy the booksellers' demands. Yet he managed to sustain a remarkable coherence of ethical ambition and personal presence throughout his voluminous labours. His twice-weekly essays for *The Rambler* (1750–52), for instance, consistently show his powers at their fullest stretch, handling an impressive array of literary and moral topics with a scrupulous intellectual gravity and attentiveness. Many of the preoccupations of *The Vanity of Human Wishes* and the *Rambler* essays reappear in *Rasselas* (1759), which catalogues with profound resource the vulnerability of human philosophies of life to humiliation at the hands of life itself.

Johnson's forensic brilliance can be seen in his relentless review of Soame Jenyns's *Free Inquiry into the Nature and Origin of Evil* (1757), which caustically dissects the latter's complacent attitude to human suffering, and his analytic capacities are evidenced at their height in the successful completion of two major projects, his innovative *Dictionary of the English Language* (1755) and the great edition of Shakespeare's plays (1765). The former of these is in some ways his greatest work of literary criticism, for it displays the uses of words by means of illustrations culled from the best writing in English. The latter played a major part in the establishment of Shakespeare as the linchpin

Oa'tmeal. *n. ſ.* [*oat* and *meal.*] Flower made by grinding oats.

Oatmeal and butter, outwardly applied, dry the ſcab on the head. *Arbuthnot on Aliment.*

Our neighbours tell me oft, in joking talk,
Of aſhes, leather, *oatmeal*, bran, and chalk. *Gay.*

Oa'tmeal. *n. ſ.* An herb. *Ainſworth.*

Oats. *n. ſ.* [aten, Saxon.] A grain, which in England is generally given to horſes, but in Scotland ſupports the people.

It is of the graſs leaved tribe; the flowers have no petals, and are diſpoſed in a looſe panicle: the grain is eatable. The meal makes tolerable good bread. *Miller.*

The *oats* have eaten the horſes. *Shakeſpeare.*

It is bare mechaniſm, no otherwiſe produced than the turning of a wild *oatbeard*, by the inſinuation of the particles of moiſture. *Locke.*

For your lean cattle, fodder them with barley ſtraw firſt, and the *oat* ſtraw laſt. *Mortimer's Huſbandry.*

His horſe's allowance of *oats* and beans, was greater than the journey required. *Swift.*

Oa'tthistle. *n. ſ.* [*oat* and *thiſtle.*] An herb. *Ainſ.*

A detail of Samuel Johnson's Dictionary of the English Language. *The definition of "Oats" is often cited as evidence of Johnson's prejudice against Scots.* Courtesy of the Newberry Library, Chicago

of a national literary canon. It should be noted, however, that Johnson's was but the most critically inspired of a series of major Shakespeare editions in the 18th century. These include editions by Nicholas Rowe (1709), Pope (1725), Lewis Theobald (1734), Sir Thomas Hanmer (1744), and William Warburton (1747). Others, by Edward Capell (1768), George Steevens (1773), and Edmund Malone (1790), would follow. Johnson was but one of those helping to form a national literature.

Johnson's last years produced much political writing including the humanely resonant *Thoughts on the Late Transactions Respecting Falkland's Islands*, 1771; the socially and historically alert *Journey to the Western Islands of Scotland*, 1775; and the consummate *Lives of the Poets,* 1779–81. The latter was the climax of 40 years' writing of poetic biographies, including the multifaceted *An Account of the Life of Mr. Richard Savage* (1744). These last lives, covering the period from Cowley to the generation of Gray, show Johnson's mastery of the biographer's art of selection and emphasis and (together with the preface and notes to his Shakespeare edition) contain the most provocative critical writing of the century.

Although his allegiances lay with Neoclassical assumptions about poetic form and language, Johnson's capacity for improvisatory responsiveness to practice that lay outside the prevailing decorums should not be underrated. His final faith, however, in his own creative practice as in his criticism, was that the greatest art eschews unnecessary particulars and aims toward carefully pondered and ambitious generalization. The same creed was eloquently expounded by another member of the Johnson circle, Sir Joshua Reynolds, in his 15 *Discourses* (delivered to the Royal Academy between 1769 and 1790, but first published collectively in 1797).

James Boswell

The other prime source of Johnson's fame, his reputation as a conversationalist of epic genius, rests on the detailed testimony of contemporary memorialists including Burney, Hester Lynch Piozzi, and Sir John Hawkins. But the key text is James Boswell's magisterial *Life of Samuel Johnson* (1791). This combines in unique measure a deep respect for its subject's ethical probity and resourceful intellect with a far from inevitably complimentary eye for the telling details of his personal habits and deportment. Boswell manifests rich dramatic talent and a precise ear for conversational rhythms in his re-creation and orchestration of the debates that lie at the heart of this great biography. Another dimension of Boswell's literary talent came to light in the 1920s and 1930s when two separate hoards of unpublished manuscripts were discovered. In these he is his own subject of study. The 18th century had not previously produced much autobiographical writing of the first rank, though the actor and playwright Colley Cibber's flamboyant *Apology for the Life of Mr. Colley Cibber* (1740) and Cowper's sombre *Memoir* (written about 1766, first published in 1816) are two notable exceptions. But the drama of Boswell's self-observations has a richer texture than either of these. In the *London Journal* especially (covering 1762–63, first published in 1950), he records the processes of his dealings with others and of his own self-imaginings with a sometimes unnerving frankness and a tough willingness to ask difficult questions of himself.

Boswell narrated his experiences at the same time as, or shortly after, they occurred. Edward Gibbon, on the other hand, taking full advantage of hindsight, left in manuscript at his death six autobiographical fragments, all having much ground in common, but each telling a subtly different version of his life. Though he was in many ways invincibly more reticent than Boswell, Gibbon's successive explorations of his own history yet form a movingly resolute effort to see the truth clearly. These writings were undertaken after the completion of the great work of his life, *The History of the Decline and Fall of the Roman Empire* (1776–88). He brought to the latter an untiring dedication in the gathering and assimilation of knowledge, an especial alertness to evidence of human fallibility and failure, and a powerful ordering intelligence supported by a delicate sense of aesthetic coherence. His central theme—that the destruction of the Roman Empire was the joint triumph of barbarism and Christianity—is sustained with formidable ironic resource.

David Garrick costumed for the title role of Shakespeare's Richard III, *engraving by William Hogarth, 1746; in the British Museum.* Courtesy of the trustees of the British Museum; photograph, J.R. Freeman & Co. Ltd.

18TH-CENTURY DRAMA

After 1710, contemporary writing for the English stage waned in vitality. The 18th century was a period of great acting and strong popular enthusiasm for the theatre, but only a few dramatists—John Gay, Henry Fielding, Oliver Goldsmith, and Richard Brinsley Sheridan—achieved writing of a quality to compete with their predecessors' best. Restoration masterpieces continued to be performed well into the 19th century, though in revised, often bowdlerized, form, and the influence of this comic tradition was also strongly apparent in satiric poetry and the novel in the decades that followed.

Gay's poetry was much influenced by that of Pope, who was a contemporary and close friend. Gay was a member, together with Pope, Swift, and Arbuthnot, of the Scriblerus Club, a literary group that aimed to ridicule pedantry. These friends contributed to two of Gay's satirical plays: *The What D'ye Call It* (1715) and *Three Hours After Marriage* (1717).

Gay's most successful play was *The Beggar's Opera*, produced in London on Jan. 29, 1728, by the theatre manager John Rich at Lincoln's Inn Fields Theatre. It ran for 62 performances (not consecutive, but the longest run then known). A story of thieves and highwaymen, it was intended to mirror the moral degradation of society and, more particularly, to caricature Sir Robert Walpole and his Whig administration. It also made fun of the prevailing fashion for Italian opera. The play was stageworthy, however, not so much because of its pungent satire but because of its effective situations and "singable" songs. The production of its sequel, *Polly*, was forbidden by the lord chamberlain (doubtless on Walpole's instructions); but the ban was an excellent advertisement for the piece, and subscriptions for copies of the printed edition made more than £1,000 profit for the author. (It was eventually produced in 1777, when it had a moderate success.) His *Beggar's Opera* was successfully transmitted into the 20th century by Bertolt Brecht and Kurt Weill as *Die Dreigroschenoper* (1928; *The Threepenny Opera*).

Fielding, who left school at age 17, was a strikingly handsome youth who settled down to the life of a young gentleman of leisure; but four years later, after an abortive elopement with an heiress and the production of a play at the Drury Lane Theatre in London, he resumed his classical studies at the University of Leiden in Holland. After 18 months he had to return home because his father was no longer able to pay him an allowance. "Having," as he said, "no choice but to be a hackney-writer or a hackney-coachman," he chose the former and set up as playwright. In all, he wrote some 25 plays. Although his dramatic works have aged poorly and are by and large not performed today, their wit cannot be denied. He was essentially a satirist; for instance, *The Author's Farce* (1730) displays the absurdities of writers and publishers, while *Rape upon Rape* (1730) satirizes the injustices of the law and lawyers. His target was often the political corruption of the times. In 1737 he produced at the Little Theatre in the Hay (later the Haymarket Theatre), London, his *Historical Register, For the Year 1736,* in which the prime minister, Sir Robert Walpole, was represented practically undisguised and mercilessly ridiculed. It was not the first time Walpole had suffered from Fielding's pen, and his answer was to push through Parliament the Licensing Act, by which all new plays had to be approved and licensed by the lord chamberlain before production. The passing of this act marked the end of Fielding's career as a playwright.

Goldsmith turned to the theatre in 1768, only after he had established himself in other fields of literary endeavour. By 1762 he had established himself as an essayist with his satirical *Citizen of the World*. By 1764 he had won a reputation as a poet with *The Traveller,* the first work to which he put his name. (He would later confirm that reputation in 1770 with the more famous *Deserted Village*.) In 1766 Goldsmith revealed himself as a novelist with *The Vicar of Wakefield* (written in 1762), a portrait of village life whose idealization of the countryside, sentimental moralizing, and melodramatic incidents are underlain by a sharp but good-natured irony. In 1768 Goldsmith turned to the theatre with *The Good Natur'd Man,* which was followed in 1773 by the much more effective *She Stoops to Conquer*, which was immediately successful. This play has outlived almost all other English-language comedies from the early 18th to the late 19th century by virtue of its broadly farcical horseplay and vivid, humorous characterizations.

Goldsmith's success as a writer lay partly in the charm of personality emanated by his style—his affection for his characters, his mischievous irony, and his spontaneous interchange of gaiety and sadness. He was, as a writer, "natural, simple, affecting." It is by their human personalities that his novel and his plays succeed, not by any brilliance of plot, ideas, or language. In these works Goldsmith helped to humanize his era's literary imagination, without growing sickly or mawkish. Goldsmith saw people, human situations, and indeed the human predicament from the comic point of view; he was a realist, something of a satirist, but in his final judgments unfailingly charitable.

Even a writer of Sheridan's undeniable resource produced in his best plays—*The Rivals*, *The School for Scandal*, and *The Critic*—writing that seems more like a technically ingenious, but cautious, rearrangement of familiar materials than a truly innovative contribution to the corpus of English comic writing for the stage. After marriage in 1773, Sheridan turned to the theatre for a livelihood. His comedy *The Rivals* opened at Covent Garden Theatre, London, in January 1775. It ran an hour longer than was usual, and, because of the offensive nature and poor acting of the character of Sir Lucius O'Trigger, it was hardly a success. Drastically revised and with a new actor as Sir Lucius, its second performance 11 days later won immediate applause. The situations and characters were not entirely new, but Sheridan gave them freshness by his rich wit, and the whole play reveals Sheridan's remarkable sense of theatrical effect. The play is characteristic of Sheridan's work in its genial mockery of the affectation displayed by some of the characters. Even the malapropisms that slow down the play give a proper sense of caricature to the character of Mrs. Malaprop.

Some of the play's success was due to the acting of Lawrence Clinch as Sir Lucius. Sheridan showed his gratitude by writing the amusing little farce *St. Patrick's Day; or,*

The Scheming Lieutenant for the benefit performance given for Clinch in May 1775. Another example of his ability to weave an interesting plot from well-worn materials is seen in *The Duenna,* produced the following November. The characters are generally undeveloped, but the intrigue of the plot and charming lyrics and the music by his father-in-law, Thomas Linley, and his son gave this ballad opera great popularity. Its 75 performances exceeded the record-setting 62 credited to Gay's *The Beggar's Opera*.

Thus, in less than a year Sheridan had brought himself to the forefront of contemporary dramatists. David Garrick, looking for someone to succeed him as manager and proprietor of Drury Lane Theatre, saw in Sheridan a young man with energy, shrewdness, and a real sense of theatre. A successful physician, James Ford, agreed with Garrick's estimate and increased his investment in the playhouse. In 1776, Sheridan and Linley became partners with Ford in a half-share of Drury Lane Theatre. Two years later they bought the other half from Willoughby Lacy, Garrick's partner.

In fact, Sheridan's interest in his theatre soon began to seem rather fitful. Nevertheless, he was responsible for the renewed appreciation of Restoration comedy that followed the revival of the plays of William Congreve at Drury Lane. In February 1777 he brought out his version of Sir John Vanbrugh's *The Relapse* (1696) as *A Trip to Scarborough,* again showing his talent for revision. He gave the rambling plot a neater shape and removed much indelicacy from the dialogue, but the result was disappointing, probably because of the loss of much of the earlier play's gusto.

What Sheridan learned from the Restoration dramatists can be seen in *The School for Scandal,* produced at Drury Lane in May 1777. That play earned him the title of "the modern Congreve." Although resembling Congreve in that its satirical wit is so brilliant and so general that it does not always distinguish one character from another, *The School for Scandal* does contain two subtle portraits in Joseph Surface and Lady Teazle. There were several Restoration models (e.g., Mrs. Pinchwife in William Wycherley's *The Country-Wife* and Miss Hoyden in Vanbrugh's *The Relapse*) for the portrayal of a country girl amazed and delighted by the sexual freedom of high society. Sheridan softened his Lady Teazle, however, to suit the more refined taste of his day. The part combined innocence and sophistication and was incomparably acted. The other parts were written with equal care to suit the members of the company, and the whole work was a triumph of intelligence and imaginative calculation. With its spirited ridicule of affectation and pretentiousness, it is often considered the greatest comedy of manners in English.

Sheridan's flair for stage effect, exquisitely demonstrated in scenes in *The School for Scandal,* was again demonstrated in his delightful satire on stage conventions, *The Critic,* which since its first performance in October 1779 has been thought much funnier than its model, *The Rehearsal* (1671), by George Villiers, the 2nd duke of Buckingham. Sheridan himself considered the first act to be his finest piece of writing. Although Puff is little more than a type, Sir Fretful Plagiary is not only a caricature of the dramatist Richard Cumberland but also an epitome of the vanity of authors in every age. The sallies against the follies of society in *The Critic*, as in his other major plays, have a polish that makes Sheridan the natural link in the history of the British comedy of manners between Congreve and the great 19th-century writer, playwright, and wit Oscar Wilde.

Comedy of Manners

The genre known as the comedy of manners is a witty, cerebral form of dramatic comedy that depicts and often satirizes the manners and affectations of a contemporary society. A comedy of manners is concerned with social usage and the question of whether or not characters meet certain social standards. Often the governing social standard is morally trivial but exacting. The plot of such a comedy, usually concerned with an illicit love affair or similarly scandalous matter, is subordinate to the play's brittle atmosphere, witty dialogue, and pungent commentary on human foibles.

The comedy of manners, which was usually written by sophisticated authors for members of their own coterie or social class, has historically thrived in periods and societies that combined material prosperity and moral latitude. Such was the case in ancient Greece when Menander (*c.* 342–*c.* 292 BCE) inaugurated New Comedy, the forerunner of comedy of manners. Menander's smooth style, elaborate plots, and stock characters were imitated by the Roman poets Plautus (*c.* 254–184 BCE) and Terence (186/185–159 bce), whose comedies were widely known and copied during the Renaissance.

One of the greatest exponents of the comedy of manners was Molière, who satirized the hypocrisy and pretension of 17th-century French society in such plays as *L'École des femmes* (1662; *The School for Wives*) and *Le Misanthrope* (1666; *The Misanthrope*).

In England the comedy of manners had its great day during the Restoration period. Although influenced by Ben Jonson's comedy of humours, the Restoration comedy of manners was lighter, defter, and more vivacious in tone. Playwrights declared themselves against affected wit and acquired follies and satirized these qualities in caricature characters with label-like names such as Sir Fopling Flutter (in Sir George Etherege's *Man of Mode,* 1676) and Tattle (in William Congreve's *The Old Batchelour,* 1693). The masterpieces of the genre were the witty, cynical, and epigrammatic plays of William Wycherley (*The Country-Wife,* 1675) and William Congreve (*The Way of the World,* 1700). In the late 18th century Oliver Goldsmith (*She Stoops to Conquer,* 1773) and Richard Brinsley Sheridan (*The Rivals*, 1775; *The School for Scandal*, 1777) revived the form.

The tradition of elaborate, artificial plotting and epigrammatic dialogue was carried on by the Anglo-Irish playwright Oscar Wilde in *Lady Windermere's Fan* (1892) and *The Importance of Being Earnest* (1895). In the 20th century the comedy of manners reappeared in the witty, sophisticated drawing-room plays of the British dramatists Noël Coward and Somerset Maugham and the Americans Philip Barry and S.N. Behrman.

CHAPTER 3

THE ROMANTIC PERIOD

As a term to cover the most distinctive writers who flourished in the last years of the 18th century and the first decades of the 19th, *Romantic* is indispensable but also a little misleading. There was no self-styled "Romantic movement" at the time, and the great writers of the period did not call themselves Romantics. Not until August Wilhelm von Schlegel's Vienna lectures of 1808–09 was a clear distinction established between the "organic," "plastic" qualities of Romantic art and the "mechanical" character of Classicism.

Many of the age's foremost writers thought that something new was happening in world affairs, nevertheless. William Blake's affirmation in 1793 that "a new heaven is begun" was matched a generation later by Percy Bysshe Shelley's "The world's great age begins anew." "These, these will give the world another heart, / And other pulses," wrote John Keats, referring to Leigh Hunt and William Wordsworth. Fresh ideals came to the fore, in particular, that freedom was being extended to every range of human endeavour. As that ideal swept through Europe, it became natural to believe the age of tyrants might soon end.

POETRY

The most notable feature of the poetry of the time is the new role of individual thought and personal feeling.

Where the main trend of 18th-century poetics had been to praise the general, to see the poet as a spokesman of society addressing a cultivated and homogeneous audience, and having as his end the conveyance of "truth," the Romantics found the source of poetry in the particular, unique experience. Blake's marginal comment on Sir Joshua Reynolds's *Discourses* expresses the position with characteristic vehemence: "To Generalize is to be an Idiot. To Particularize is the alone Distinction of Merit." The poet was seen as an individual distinguished from his fellows by the intensity of his perceptions, taking as his basic subject matter the workings of his own mind. Poetry was regarded as conveying its own truth; sincerity was the criterion by which it was to be judged.

The emphasis on feeling—seen perhaps at its finest in the poems of Robert Burns—was in some ways a continuation of the earlier "cult of sensibility"; it is worth remembering that Alexander Pope praised his father as having known no language but the language of the heart. But feeling had begun to receive particular emphasis and is found in most of the Romantic definitions of poetry. Wordsworth called poetry "the spontaneous overflow of powerful feeling," and in 1833 John Stuart Mill defined poetry as "feeling itself, employing thought only as the medium of its utterance." It followed that the best poetry was that in which the greatest intensity of feeling was expressed, and hence a new importance was attached to the lyric.

Another key quality of Romantic writing was its shift from the mimetic, or imitative, assumptions of the Neoclassical era to a new stress on imagination. Samuel Taylor Coleridge saw the imagination as the supreme poetic quality, a quasi-divine creative force that made the poet a godlike being. Samuel Johnson had seen the components of poetry as "invention, imagination and judgement," but Blake wrote: "One Power alone makes a Poet: Imagination, the Divine Vision." The poets of this period accordingly placed great emphasis on the workings of the unconscious mind, on dreams and reveries, on the supernatural, and on the childlike or primitive view of the world, this last being regarded as valuable because its clarity and intensity had not been overlaid by the restrictions of civilized "reason." Rousseau's sentimental conception of the "noble savage" was often invoked, and often by those who were ignorant that the phrase is Dryden's or that the type was adumbrated in the "poor Indian" of Pope's *An Essay on Man*.

A further sign of the diminished stress placed on judgment is the Romantic attitude to form. If poetry must be spontaneous, sincere, intense, it should be fashioned primarily according to the dictates of the creative imagination. Wordsworth advised a young poet, "You feel strongly; trust to those feelings, and your poem will take its shape and proportions as a tree does from the vital principle that actuates it." This organic view of poetry is opposed to the classical theory of "genres," each with its own linguistic decorum; and it led to the feeling that poetic sublimity was unattainable except in short passages.

Hand in hand with the new conception of poetry and the insistence on a new subject matter went a demand for new ways of writing. Wordsworth and his followers, particularly Keats, found the prevailing poetic diction of the late 18th century stale and stilted, or "gaudy and inane," and totally unsuited to the expression of their perceptions. It could not be, for them, the language of feeling, and Wordsworth accordingly sought to bring the language of poetry back to that of common speech. Wordsworth's own diction, however, often differs from his theory. Nevertheless, when he published his preface to *Lyrical Ballads* in 1800, the time was ripe for a change: the flexible diction of earlier 18th-century poetry had hardened into a merely conventional language.

The Lake Poets

The poets William Wordsworth, Samuel Taylor Coleridge, and Robert Southey were first described derogatorily as the "Lake school" by Francis (afterward Lord) Jeffrey in *The Edinburgh Review* in August 1817, and the description "Lakers" was also used in a similar spirit by the poet Lord Byron. These names confusingly group Wordsworth and Coleridge together with Southey, who did not subscribe in his views or work to their theories of poetry. All three poets lived in the English Lake District of Cumberland and Westmorland (now Cumbria) at the beginning of the 19th century.

The Major Romantic Poets

Useful as it is to trace the common elements in Romantic poetry, there was little conformity among the poets themselves. It is misleading to read the poetry of the first Romantics as if it had been written primarily to express their feelings. The concern of Blake, Wordsworth, and Coleridge was, rather, to change the intellectual climate of the age. The poets of the next generation—Keats, Shelley, and Byron—shared their predecessors' passion for liberty (now set in a new perspective by the French revolutionary and Napoleonic wars) and were in a position to learn from their experiments.

William Blake

William Blake's profession was engraving, and his principal avocation was painting in watercolours. But even from boyhood he wrote poetry. Born in 1757, he attended the literary and artistic salons of the bluestocking Harriet Mathew in the early 1780s, and there he read and sang his poems. According to Blake's friend John Thomas Smith,

"He was listened to by the company with profound silence, and allowed [. . .] to possess original and extraordinary merit." In 1783 Harriet Mathew's husband, the Rev. Anthony Stephen Mathew, and Blake's friend John Flaxman had some of these poems printed in a modest little volume of 70 pages titled *Poetical Sketches*, with the attribution on the title page reading simply, "By W.B." It contained an "advertisement" by Reverend Mathew that

William Blake was by profession an engraver, not a poet, and he showed little interest in having his poetry published during his lifetime. Today, he is considered one of the leading figures among the Romantic poets. Hulton Archive/Getty Images

stated, "Conscious of the irregularities and defects to be found in almost every page, his friends have still believed that they possessed a poetic originality which merited some respite from oblivion." They gave the sheets of the book, uncut and unsewn, to Blake, in the expectation that he would sell them or at least give them away to potential patrons. Blake, however, showed little interest in the volume, and when he died he still had uncut and unstitched copies in his possession.

But some contemporaries and virtually all succeeding critics agreed that the poems did merit "respite from oblivion." Some are merely boyish rodomontade, but some, such as *To Winter* and *Mad Song*, are exquisite. *To the Muses*, lamenting the death of music, concludes,

How have you left the antient love
That bards of old enjoy'd in you!
The languid strings do scarcely move!
The sound is forc'd, the notes are few!

Eighty-five years later, Algernon Charles Swinburned wrote that in these lines "The Eighteenth Century died to music."

Blake never published his poetry in the ordinary way. Instead, using a technology revealed to him by his brother Robert in a vision, he drew his poems and their surrounding designs on copper in a liquid impervious to acid. He then etched them and, with the aid of his devoted wife, printed them, coloured them, stitched them in rough sugar-paper wrappers, and offered them for sale. He rarely printed more than a dozen copies at a time, reprinting them when his stock ran low, and no more than 30 copies of any of them survive. Several are known only in unique copies, and some to which he refers no longer exist.

After experimenting with tiny plates to print his short tracts *There Is No Natural Religion* (1788) and *All Religions Are One* (1788?), Blake created the first of the poetical works for which he is chiefly remembered: *Songs of Innocence*, with 19 poems on 26 prints. The poems are written for children—in *Infant Joy* only three words have as many as two syllables—and they represent the innocent and the vulnerable, from babies to beetles, protected and fostered by powers beyond their own. In *The Chimney Sweeper*, for example,

[. . .]the Angel told Tom if he'd be a good boy,
He'd have God for his father & never want joy.
And so Tom awoke and we rose in the dark
And got with our bags & our brushes to work.
Tho' the morning was cold, Tom was happy & warm.
So if all do their duty, they need not fear harm.

Sustained by the vision, "Tom was happy & warm" despite the cold.

In one of the best-known lyrics, called *The Lamb*, a little boy gives to a lamb the same kind of catechism he himself had been given in church:

Little Lamb, who made thee?
Dost thou know who made thee?
. . .
Little Lamb, I'll tell thee,
Little Lamb, I'll tell thee:
He is called by thy name,
For he calls himself a Lamb
. . .
I a child, & thou a lamb,
We are called by his name.

The syllogism is simple if not simplistic: the creator of child and lamb has the same qualities as his creation.

Most of Blake's poetry embodies myths that he invented. Blake takes the inquiry about the nature of life a little further in *The Book of Thel* (1789), the first of his published myths. The melancholy shepherdess Thel asks, "Why fade these children of the spring? Born but to smile & fall." She is answered by the Lilly of the Valley (representing water), the Cloud (air), and the Clod of Clay (earth), who tell her, "we live not for ourselves," and say that they are nourished by "he that loves the lowly." Thel enters the "land unknown" and hears a "voice of sorrow":

"Why cannot the Ear be closed to its own destruction?
Or the glistning Eye to the poison of a smile!"

The poem concludes with the frightened Thel seeing her own grave there, shrieking, and fleeing back to her valley.

Blake's *The Marriage of Heaven and Hell* (1790?) has become one of his best known. It is a prose work in no familiar form; for instance, on the title page, no author, printer, or publisher is named. It is in part a parody of Emanuel Swedenborg, echoing the Swedish theologian's "Memorable Relations" of things seen and heard in heaven with "Memorable Fancies" of things seen and heard in hell. The section titled "Proverbs of Hell" eulogizes energy with lines such as "Energy is Eternal Delight," "Exuberance is Beauty," and "The road of excess leads to the palace of wisdom." The work ends with "A Song of Liberty," which celebrates the values of those who stormed the Bastille in 1789: "Let the Priests of the Raven of dawn, no longer [. . .] curse the sons of joy [. . .] For every thing that lives is Holy."

America, A Prophecy (1793) and *Europe, A Prophecy* (1794) are even more daringly political, and they are boldly acknowledged on the title pages as "Printed by William Blake." In the first, Albion's Angel, representing the reactionary government of England, perceives Orc, the spirit of energy, as a "Blasphemous Demon, Antichrist, hater of Dignities," but Orc's vision is of an apocalypse that transforms the world:

Let the slave grinding at the mill, run out into the field,
Let him look up into the heavens & laugh in the bright air;
. . .
For Empire is no more, and now the Lion & Wolf shall cease
. . .
For every thing that lives is holy

The mental revolution seems to be accomplished, but the design for the triumphant concluding page shows not rejoicing and triumph but barren trees, bowed mourners, thistles, and serpents. Blake's designs often tell a complementary story, and the two visions must be combined in the reader's mind to comprehend the meaning of the work.

The frontispiece to *Europe* is one of Blake's best-known images: sometimes called *The Ancient of Days*, it represents a naked, bearded old man leaning out from the sun to define the universe with golden compasses. He seems a familiar image of God, but the usual notions about this deity are challenged by an image, on the facing title page, of what the God of reason has created: a coiling serpent with open mouth and forked tongue. It seems to represent how

Thought chang'd the infinite to a serpent; that which pitieth:
To a devouring flame; and man fled from its face [. . .]
. . .

Then was the serpent temple form'd, image of infinite
Shut up in finite revolutions, and man became an Angel;
Heaven a mighty circle turning; God a tyrant crown'd.

This God is opposed by Orc and by Los, the imagination, and at the end of the poem Los "call'd all his sons to the strife of blood." The work's last illustration, however, is not of the heroic sons of Los storming the barricades of tyrannical reason but of a naked man carrying a fainting woman and a terrified girl from the horrors of a burning city.

In the same year as *Europe*, Blake published *Songs of Experience* and combined it with his previous lyrics to form *Songs of Innocence and of Experience Shewing the Two Contrary States of the Human Soul*. The poems of *Songs of Experience* centre on threatened, unprotected souls in despair. In *London* the speaker, shown in the design as blind, bearded, and "age-bent," sees in "every face . . . marks of woe," and observes that "In every voice . . . The mind-forg'd manacles I hear." In *The Tyger*, which answers *The Lamb of Innocence*, the despairing speaker asks the "Tyger burning bright" about its creator: "Did he who made the Lamb make thee?" But in the design the "deadly terrors" of the text are depicted as a small, meek animal often coloured more like a stuffed toy than a jungle beast.

Blake's most impressive writings are his enormous prophecies *Vala or The Four Zoas* (which Blake composed and revised from roughly 1796 to 1807 but never published), *Milton*, and *Jerusalem: The Emanation of the Giant Albion*. In them, his myth expands, adding to Urizen (reason) and Los (imagination) the Zoas Tharmas and Luvah. (The word *zoa* is a Greek plural meaning "living creatures.") Their primordial harmony is destroyed when each of them attempts to fix creation in a form corresponding to his own nature and genius. Blake describes his purpose, his "great task," in *Jerusalem*:

To open the immortal Eyes
Of man inwards into the worlds of thought; into Eternity
Ever expanding in the Bosom of God, the Human Imagination.

Like the Zoa Los, Blake felt that he must "Create a System or be enslav'd by another Mans."

Milton concerns Blake's attempt, at Milton's request, to correct the ideas of *Paradise Lost*. The poem originated in an event in Felpham, recorded in Blake's letters, in which the spirit of Milton as a falling star entered Blake. It includes the lyric commonly called "Jerusalem" that has become a kind of alternative national anthem in Britain:

I will not cease from Mental Fight,
Nor shall my Sword sleep in my hand:
Till we have built Jerusalem,
In Englands green & pleasant Land.

Visions were commonplaces to Blake, and his life and works were intensely spiritual. His friend the journalist Henry Crabb Robinson wrote that when Blake was four years old he saw God's head appear in a window. While still a child he also saw the Prophet Ezekiel under a tree in the fields and had a vision, according to his first biographer, Alexander Gilchrist (1828–61), of "a tree filled with angels, bright angelic wings bespangling every bough like stars." Robinson reported in his diary that Blake spoke of visions "in the ordinary unemphatic tone in which we speak of trivial matters. . . . Of the faculty of Vision he spoke as One he had had from early infancy—He thinks all men partake of it—but it is lost by not being cultiv[ate]d." In his essay *A Vision of the Last Judgment,* Blake wrote:

I assert for My Self that I do not behold the outward Creation . . . 'What' it will be Questiond 'When the Sun rises, do you not See a round Disk of fire somewhat like a Guinea?' O no no I see an Innumerable company of the Heavenly host crying 'Holy Holy Holy is the Lord God Almighty!'

Blake wrote to his patron William Hayley in 1802, "I am under the direction of Messengers from Heaven Daily & Nightly." These visions were the source of many of his poems and drawings. As he wrote in his *Auguries of Innocence*, his purpose was

To see a World in a Grain of Sand
And a Heaven in a Wild Flower
Hold Infinity in the palm of your hand
And Eternity in an hour.

He was, he wrote in 1804, "really drunk with intellectual vision whenever I take a pencil or graver into my hand." Blake's wife once said to his young friend Seymour Kirkup, "I have very little of Mr. Blake's company; he is always in Paradise."

Some of this stress on visions may have been fostered by his mother, who, with her first husband, had become a Moravian when the group was in its most intensely emotional and visionary phase. In her letter of 1750 applying to join the Moravians, she wrote that "last Friday at the love feast Our Savour [sic] was pleased to make me Suck his wounds."

WILLIAM WORDSWORTH

William Wordsworth was born in 1770 in the Lake District of northern England, the second of five children of a modestly prosperous estate manager. His mother died when he was 7, and his father died when he was 13, upon which the orphan boys were sent off by guardian uncles to a grammar school at Hawkshead, a village in the heart of the Lake District. At Hawkshead Wordsworth received an excellent education in classics, literature, and mathematics, but the chief advantage to him there was the chance to indulge in the boyhood pleasures of living and playing in the outdoors. The natural scenery of the English lakes could terrify as well as nurture, as Wordsworth would later

William Wordsworth, portrait by Henry Eldridge, 1804; in Dove Cottage, Grasmere, Eng. Courtesy of the trustees of Dove Cottage, Grasmere, Eng.; photograph, Sanderson and Dixon, Ltd.

testify in the line "I grew up fostered alike by beauty and by fear." Yet its generally benign aspect gave the growing boy the confidence he articulated in one of his first important poems, "Lines Composed a Few Miles Above Tintern Abbey . . .," namely, "that Nature never did betray the heart that loved her."

Wordsworth moved on in 1787 to St. John's College, Cambridge. Repelled by the competitive pressures there, he elected to idle his way through the university, persuaded that he "was not for that hour, nor for that place." The most important thing he did in his college years was to devote his summer vacation in 1790 to a long walking tour through revolutionary France. There he was caught up in the passionate enthusiasm that followed the fall of the Bastille, and became an ardent republican sympathizer. Upon taking his Cambridge degree—an undistinguished "pass"—he returned in 1791 to France, where he formed a passionate attachment to a Frenchwoman, Annette Vallon. But before their child was born in December 1792, Wordsworth had to return to England and was cut off there by the outbreak of war between England and France. He was not to see his daughter Caroline until she was nine.

The three or four years that followed his return to England were the darkest of Wordsworth's life. Unprepared for any profession, rootless, virtually penniless, bitterly hostile to his own country's opposition to the French, he lived in London in the company of radicals like William Godwin and learned to feel a profound sympathy for the abandoned mothers, beggars, children, vagrants, and victims of England's wars who began to march through the sombre poems he began writing at this time. This dark period ended in 1795, when a friend's legacy made possible Wordsworth's reunion with his beloved sister Dorothy—the two were never again to live apart—and their move in 1797 to Alfoxden House, near

Bristol. There Wordsworth became friends with a fellow poet, Samuel Taylor Coleridge, and they formed a partnership that would change both poets' lives and alter the course of English poetry.

Their partnership, rooted in one marvelous year (1797–98) in which they "together wantoned in wild Poesy," had two consequences for Wordsworth. First it turned him away from the long poems on which he had laboured since his Cambridge days. These included poems of social protest like *Salisbury Plain,* loco-descriptive poems such as *An Evening Walk* and *Descriptive Sketches* (published in 1793), and *The Borderers,* a blank-verse tragedy exploring the psychology of guilt (and not published until 1842). Stimulated by Coleridge and under the healing influences of nature and his sister, Wordsworth began in 1797–98 to compose the short lyrical and dramatic poems for which he is best remembered by many readers. Some of these were affectionate tributes to Dorothy, some were tributes to daffodils, birds, and other elements of "Nature's holy plan," and some were portraits of simple rural people intended to illustrate basic truths of human nature.

Many of these short poems were written to a daringly original program formulated jointly by Wordsworth and Coleridge, and aimed at breaking the decorum of Neoclassical verse. These poems appeared in 1798 in a slim, anonymously authored volume entitled *Lyrical Ballads,* which opened with Coleridge's long poem *The Rime of the Ancient Mariner* and closed with Wordsworth's "Tintern Abbey." All but three of the intervening poems were Wordsworth's, and, as he declared in a preface to a second edition two years later, their object was "to choose incidents and situations from common life and to relate or describe them . . . in a selection of language really used by men, . . . tracing in them . . . the primary laws of our nature." Most of the poems were dramatic in form, designed to reveal the character of the speaker. The manifesto and the accompanying poems thus set forth a new style, a new vocabulary, and new subjects for poetry. If not itself solely responsible for doing so, *Lyrical Ballads* helped launch the English Romantic movement.

The second consequence of Wordsworth's partnership with Coleridge was the framing of a vastly ambitious poetic design that teased and haunted him for the rest of his life. Coleridge had projected an enormous poem to be called "The Brook," in which he proposed to treat all science, philosophy, and religion, but he soon laid the burden of writing this poem upon Wordsworth himself. As early as 1798 Wordsworth began to talk in grand terms of this poem, to be entitled *The Recluse*. To nerve himself up to this enterprise and to test his powers, Wordsworth began writing the autobiographical poem that would absorb him intermittently for the next 40 years, and which was eventually published in 1850 under the title *The Prelude, or, Growth of a Poet's Mind*. *The Prelude* extends the quiet autobiographical mode of reminiscence that Wordsworth had begun in "Tintern Abbey" and traces the poet's life from his school days through his university life and his visits to France, up to the year (1799) in which he settled at Grasmere. It thus describes a circular journey—what has been called a long journey home. But the main events in the autobiography are internal: the poem exultantly describes the ways in which the imagination emerges as the dominant faculty, exerting its control over the reason and the world of the senses alike.

The Recluse itself was never completed, and only one of its three projected parts was actually written; this was published in 1814 as *The Excursion* and consisted of nine long philosophical monologues spoken by pastoral characters. The first monologue (Book I) contained a version of one of Wordsworth's greatest poems, "The Ruined

Cottage," composed in superb blank verse in 1797. This bleak narrative records the slow, pitiful decline of a woman whose husband had gone off to the army and never returned. For later versions of this poem Wordsworth added a reconciling conclusion, but the earliest and most powerful version was starkly tragic.

In the company of Dorothy, Wordsworth spent the winter of 1798–99 in Germany, where, in the remote town of Goslar, in Saxony, he experienced the most intense isolation he had ever known. As a consequence, however, he wrote some of his most moving poetry, including the "Lucy" and "Matthew" elegies and early drafts toward *The Prelude*. Upon his return to England, Wordsworth incorporated several new poems in the second edition of *Lyrical Ballads* (1800), notably two tragic pastorals of country life, "The Brothers" and "Michael." These poems, together with the brilliant lyrics that were assembled in Wordsworth's second verse collection, *Poems, in Two Volumes* (1807), help to make up what is now recognized as his great decade, stretching from his meeting with Coleridge in 1797 until 1808.

One portion of a second part of *The Recluse* was finished in 1806, but, like *The Prelude,* was left in manuscript at the poet's death. This portion, *Home at Grasmere,* joyously celebrated Wordsworth's taking possession (in December 1799) of Dove Cottage, at Grasmere, Westmorland, where he was to reside for eight of his most productive years. In 1802, during the short-lived Peace of Amiens, Wordsworth returned briefly to France, where at Calais he met his daughter and made his peace with Annette. He then returned to England to marry Mary Hutchinson, a childhood friend, and start an English family, which had grown to three sons and two daughters by 1810.

In 1805 the drowning of Wordsworth's favorite brother, John, the captain of a sailing vessel, gave Wordsworth the strongest shock he had ever experienced. "A deep distress hath humanized my Soul," he lamented in his "Elegiac Stanzas" on Peele Castle. Henceforth he would produce a different kind of poetry, defined by a new sobriety, a new restraint, and a lofty, almost Miltonic elevation of tone and diction. Wordsworth appeared to anticipate this turn in "Tintern Abbey," where he had learned to hear "the still, sad music of humanity," and again in the "Ode: Intimations of Immortality" (written in 1802–04; published in *Poems, in Two Volumes*). The theme of this ode is the loss of his power to see the things he had once seen, the radiance, the "celestial light" that seemed to lie over the landscapes of his youth like "the glory and freshness of a dream." Now, in the Peele Castle stanzas, he sorrowfully looked back on the light as illusory, as a "Poet's dream," as "the light that never was, on sea or land."

These metaphors point up the differences between the early and the late Wordsworth. It is generally accepted that the quality of his verse fell off as he grew more distant from the sources of his inspiration and as his Anglican and Tory sentiments hardened into orthodoxy. Today many readers discern two Wordsworths, the young Romantic revolutionary and the aging Tory humanist, risen into what John Keats called the "Egotistical Sublime." Little of Wordsworth's later verse matches the best of his earlier years.

In his middle period Wordsworth invested a good deal of his creative energy in odes, the best known of which is "On the Power of Sound." He also produced a large number of sonnets, most of them strung together in sequences. The most admired are the Duddon sonnets (1820), which trace the progress of a stream through Lake District landscapes and blend nature poetry with philosophic reflection in a manner now recognized as the best of the later Wordsworth. Other sonnet sequences record his tours through the European continent, and the three series of *Ecclesiastical Sketches* (1822) develop meditations, many sharply satirical, on church history. But the most memorable poems of Wordsworth's middle and late years were often cast in elegiac mode. They range from the poet's heartfelt laments for two of his children who died in 1812—laments incorporated in *The Excursion*—to brilliant lyrical effusions on the deaths of his fellow poets James Hogg, George Crabbe, Coleridge, and Charles Lamb.

In 1808 Wordsworth and his family moved from Dove Cottage to larger quarters in Grasmere, and five years later they settled at Rydal Mount, near Ambleside, where Wordsworth spent the remainder of his life. In 1813 he accepted the post of distributor of stamps for the county of Westmorland, an appointment that carried the salary of £400 a year. Wordsworth continued to hold back from publication *The Prelude*, *Home at Grasmere*, *The Borderers*, and *Salisbury Plain*. He did publish *Poems, in Two Volumes* in 1807; *The Excursion* in 1814, containing the only finished portions of *The Recluse;* and the collected *Poems* of 1815, which contained most of his shorter poems and two important critical essays as well. Wordsworth's other works published during middle age include *The White Doe of Rylstone* (1815), a poem about the pathetic shattering of a Roman Catholic family during an unsuccessful rebellion against Elizabeth I in 1569; a *Thanksgiving Ode* (1816); and *Peter Bell* (1819), a poem written in 1798 and then modulated in successive rewritings into an experiment in Romantic irony and the mock-heroic and coloured by the poet's feelings of affinity with his hero, a "wild and woodland rover." *The Waggoner* (1819) is another extended ballad about a North Country itinerant.

Throughout these years Wordsworth was assailed by vicious and tireless critical attacks by contemptuous reviewers; no great poet has ever had to endure worse.

But finally, with the publication of *The River Duddon* in 1820, the tide began to turn, and by the mid-1830s his reputation had been established with both critics and the reading public.

Wordsworth's last years were given over partly to "tinkering" his poems, as the family called his compulsive and persistent habit of revising his earlier poems through edition after edition. *The Prelude,* for instance, went through four distinct manuscript versions (1798–99, 1805–06, 1818–20, and 1832–39) and was published only after the poet's death in 1850. Most readers find the earliest versions of *The Prelude* and other heavily revised poems to be the best, but flashes of brilliance can appear in revisions added when the poet was in his seventies.

Wordsworth succeeded his friend Robert Southey as Britain's poet laureate in 1843 and held that post until his own death in 1850. Thereafter his influence was felt throughout the rest of the 19th century, though he was honoured more for his smaller poems, as singled out by the Victorian critic Matthew Arnold, than for his masterpiece, *The Prelude*. In the 20th century his reputation was strengthened both by recognition of his importance in the Romantic movement and by an appreciation of the darker elements in his personality and verse.

As the central figure in the English Romantic revolution in poetry, Wordsworth's contribution to the movement was threefold. First, he formulated in his poems and his essays a new attitude toward nature. This was more than a matter of introducing nature imagery into his verse. It amounted to a fresh view of the organic relation between man and the natural world, and it culminated in metaphors of a wedding between nature and the human mind, and beyond that, in the sweeping metaphor of nature as emblematic of the mind of God, a mind that "feeds upon infinity" and "broods over the dark abyss."

Second, he probed deeply into his own sensibility as he traced, in his finest poem, *The Prelude,* the "growth of a poet's mind." *The Prelude* was in fact the first long autobiographical poem. Writing it in a drawn-out process of self-exploration, Wordsworth worked his way toward a modern psychological understanding of his own nature, and thus more broadly of human nature. Third, Wordsworth placed poetry at the centre of human experience; in impassioned rhetoric he pronounced poetry to be nothing less than "the first and last of all knowledge—it is as immortal as the heart of man," and he then went on to create some of the greatest English poetry of his century. It is probably safe to say that by the late 20th century he stood in critical estimation where Coleridge and Arnold had originally placed him, next to John Milton—who stands, of course, next to William Shakespeare.

Dorothy Wordsworth

(b. Dec. 25, 1771, Cockermouth, Cumberland, Eng.—d. Jan. 25, 1855, Rydal Mount, Westmorland)

The *Alfoxden Journal 1798* and *Grasmere Journals 1800–03* of English prose writer Dorothy Wordsworth are read today for the imaginative power of their description of nature and for the light they throw on her brother, the poet William Wordsworth.

Their mother's death in 1778 separated Dorothy from her brothers, and from 1783 they were without a family home. The sympathy between William and Dorothy was strong. She understood him as no one else could and provided the "quickening influence" he needed. When, in 1795, he was lent a house in Dorset, she made a home for him there. At Alfoxden, Somerset, in 1796–98, she enjoyed with Wordsworth and Samuel Taylor Coleridge a companionship of "three persons with one soul."

She went with them to Germany (1798–99), and in December 1799 she and William settled for the first time in a home of their own, Dove Cottage, Grasmere, in the Lake District, remaining there after his marriage (1802) and move with the family to Rydal Mount in 1813.

In 1829 Dorothy was dangerously ill and thenceforth was obliged to lead the life of an invalid. Her ill health affected her intellect, and during the last 20 years of her life her mind was clouded.

The *Alfoxden Journal* (of which only the period from January to April 1798 survives) is a record of William's friendship with Coleridge that resulted in their *Lyrical Ballads* (1798), with which the Romantic movement began. The *Grasmere Journals* contains material on which William drew for his poetry (notably her description of daffodils in April 1802, which inspired his *I Wandered Lonely as a Cloud*). Her other surviving journals include accounts of her trip to Germany in 1798–99 as well as visits to Scotland (1803) and Switzerland (1820). None of Dorothy's writings was published in her lifetime.

SAMUEL TAYLOR COLERIDGE

Samuel Taylor Coleridge's father was vicar of Ottery and headmaster of the local grammar school. Born in 1772, Coleridge was already a prodigious reader as a child, and he immersed himself to the point of morbid fascination in romances and Eastern tales such as *The Arabian Nights' Entertainments.* In 1781 his father died suddenly, and in the following year Coleridge entered Christ's Hospital in London, where he completed his secondary education. In 1791 he entered Jesus College, Cambridge. At both school and university he continued to read voraciously, particularly in works of imagination and visionary philosophy, and he was remembered by his schoolmates for his eloquence and prodigious memory. In his third year at Cambridge, oppressed by financial difficulties, he went to

Samuel Taylor Coleridge, detail of an oil painting by Washington Allston, 1814; in the National Portrait Gallery, London. Courtesy of the National Portrait Gallery, London

London and enlisted as a dragoon under the assumed name of Silas Tomkyn Comberbache. Despite his unfitness for the life, he remained until discovered by his friends; he was then bought out by his brothers and restored to Cambridge.

Early Life and Works

On his return, Coleridge was restless. The intellectual and political turmoil surrounding the French Revolution had set in motion intense and urgent discussion concerning the nature of society. He now conceived the design of circumventing the disastrous violence that had destroyed the idealism of the French Revolution by establishing a small society that should organize itself and educate its children according to better principles than those obtaining in the society around them. A chance meeting with the poet Robert Southey led the two men to plan such a "pantisocracy" and to set up a community by the Susquehanna River in Pennsylvania. To this end Coleridge left Cambridge for good and set up with Southey as a public lecturer in Bristol. In October 1795 he married Sara Fricker, daughter of a local schoolmistress, swayed partly by Southey's suggestion that he was under an obligation to her since she had been refusing the advances of other men.

Shortly afterward, Southey defected from the pantisocratic scheme, leaving Coleridge married to a woman whom he did not really love. In a sense his career never fully recovered from this blow. If there is a makeshift quality about many of its later events, one explanation can be found in his constant need to reconcile his intellectual aspirations with the financial needs of his family. During this period, however, Coleridge's intellect flowered in an extraordinary manner, as he embarked on an investigation of the nature of the human mind, joined by William Wordsworth, with whom he had become acquainted in 1795. Together they entered upon one of the most influential creative periods of English literature. Coleridge's intellectual ebullience and his belief in the existence of a powerful "life consciousness" in all individuals rescued Wordsworth from the depression into which recent events had cast him and made possible the new approach to nature that characterized his contributions to *Lyrical Ballads* (which was to be published in 1798).

Coleridge, meanwhile, was developing a new, informal mode of poetry in which he could use a conversational tone and rhythm to give unity to a poem. Of these poems, the most successful is "Frost at Midnight," which begins with the description of a silent frosty night in Somerset and proceeds through a meditation on the relationship between the quiet work of frost and the quiet breathing of the sleeping baby at the poet's side, to conclude in a resolve that his child shall be brought up as a "child of nature," so that the sympathies that the poet has come to detect may be reinforced throughout the child's education.

At the climax of the poem, he touches another theme, which lies at the root of his philosophical attitude:

. . . so shalt thou see and hear
The lovely shapes and sounds intelligible
Of that eternal language, which thy God
Utters, who from eternity doth teach
Himself in all, and all things in himself.

Coleridge's attempts to learn this "language" and trace it through the ancient traditions of mankind also led him during this period to return to the visionary interests of his schooldays: as he ransacked works of comparative religion and mythology, he was exploring the possibility that all religions and mythical traditions, with their general agreement on the unity of God and the immortality of the soul, sprang from a universal life consciousness, which was expressed particularly through the phenomena of human genius.

While these speculations were at their most intense, he retired to a lonely farmhouse near Culbone, Somersetshire, and, according to his own account, composed under the influence of laudanum the mysterious poetic fragment known as "Kubla Khan." The exotic imagery and rhythmic chant of this poem have led many critics to conclude that it should be read as a "meaningless reverie" and enjoyed merely for its vivid and sensuous qualities. An examination of the poem in the light of Coleridge's psychological and mythological interests, however, suggests that it has, after all, a complex structure of meaning and is basically a poem about the nature of human genius. The first two stanzas show the two sides of what Coleridge elsewhere calls "commanding genius": its creative aspirations in time of peace as symbolized in the projected pleasure dome and gardens of the first stanza; and its destructive power in time of turbulence as symbolized in the wailing woman, the destructive fountain, and the voices prophesying war of the second stanza. In the final stanza the poet writes of a state of "absolute genius" in which, if inspired by a visionary "Abyssinian maid," he would become endowed with the creative, divine power of a sun god—an Apollo or Osiris subduing all around him to harmony by the fascination of his spell.

Coleridge was enabled to explore the same range of themes less egotistically in *The Rime of the Ancient Mariner*, composed during the autumn and winter of 1797–98. For this, his most famous poem, he drew upon the ballad form. The main narrative tells how a sailor who has committed a crime against the life principle by slaying an albatross suffers from torments, physical and mental, in which the nature of his crime is made known to him. The underlying life power against which he has transgressed is envisaged as a power corresponding to the influx of the sun's energy into all living creatures, thereby binding them together in a joyful communion. By killing the bird that hovered near the ship, the mariner has destroyed one of the links in this process. His own consciousness is consequently affected:

the sun, previously glorious, is seen as a bloody sun, and the energies of the deep are seen as corrupt:

All in a hot and copper sky,
The bloody Sun, at noon,
Right up above the mast did stand,
No bigger than the Moon.
. . .
The very deep did rot; O Christ!
That ever this should be!
Yea, slimy things did crawl with legs
Upon the slimy sea.
Only at night do these energies display a sinister beauty.
About, about, in reel and rout
The death-fires danced at night;
The water, like a witch's oils,
Burnt green, and blue and white.

After the death of his shipmates, alone and becalmed, devoid of a sense of movement or even of time passing, the mariner is in a hell created by the absence of any link with life. Eventually, however, a chance sight of water snakes flashing like golden fire in the darkness, answered by an outpouring of love from his heart, reinitiates the creative process. He is given a brief vision of the inner unity of the universe, in which all living things hymn their source in an interchange of harmonies. Restored to his native land, he remains haunted by what he has experienced but is at least delivered from nightmare, able to see the ordinary processes of human life with a new sense of their wonder and mercifulness.

These last qualities are reflected in the poem's attractive combination of vividness and sensitivity. The placing of it at the beginning of *Lyrical Ballads* was evidently

An illustration from a 19th-century edition of Samuel Taylor Coleridge's Rime of the Ancient Mariner, *showing the mariner made to wear the fateful albatross hung around his neck.* Time & Life Pictures/Getty Images

intended to provide a context for the sense of wonder in common life that marks many of Wordsworth's contributions. While this volume was going through the press, Coleridge began a complementary poem, a Gothic ballad entitled "Christabel," in which he aimed to show how naked energy might be redeemed through contact with a spirit of innocent love.

Troubled Years

Early in 1798 Coleridge had again found himself preoccupied with political issues. The French Revolutionary government had suppressed the states of the Swiss Confederation, and Coleridge expressed his bitterness at this betrayal of the principles of the Revolution in a poem entitled "France: An Ode."

At this time the brothers Josiah and Thomas Wedgwood, who were impressed by Coleridge's intelligence and promise, offered him in 1798 an annuity of £150 as a means of subsistence while he pursued his intellectual concerns. He used his new independence to visit Germany with Wordsworth and Wordsworth's sister, Dorothy. While there Coleridge attended lectures on physiology and biblical criticism at Göttingen. He thus became aware of developments in German scholarship that were little-known in England until many years later.

On his return to England, the tensions of his marriage were exacerbated when he fell in love with Sara Hutchinson, the sister of Wordsworth's future wife, at the end of 1799. His devotion to the Wordsworths in general did little to help matters, and for some years afterward Coleridge was troubled by domestic strife, accompanied by the worsening of his health and by his increasing dependence on opium. His main literary achievements during the period included another section of "Christabel." In 1802 Coleridge's domestic unhappiness gave rise to "Dejection: An Ode," originally a longer verse letter sent to Sara Hutchinson in which he lamented the corrosive effect of his intellectual activities when undertaken as a refuge from the lovelessness of his family life. The poem employs the technique of his conversational poems; the sensitive rhythms and phrasing that he had learned to use in them are here masterfully deployed to represent his own depressed state of mind.

Although Coleridge hoped to combine a platonic love for Sara with fidelity to his wife and children and to draw sustenance from the Wordsworth household, his hopes were not realized, and his health deteriorated further. He therefore resolved to spend some time in a warmer climate and, late in 1804, accepted a post in Malta as secretary to the acting governor. Later he spent a long time journeying across Italy, but, despite his hopes, his health did not improve during his time abroad. The time spent in Malta had been a time of personal reappraisal, however. Brought into direct contact with men accustomed to handling affairs of state, he had found himself lacking an equal forcefulness and felt that in consequence he often forfeited the respect of others. On his return to England he resolved to become more manly and decisive. Within a few months he had finally decided to separate from his wife and to live for the time being with the Wordsworths. Southey atoned for his disastrous youthful advice by exercising a general oversight of Coleridge's family for the rest of his days.

Coleridge published a periodical, *The Friend,* from June 1809 to March 1810 and ceased only when Sara Hutchinson, who had been acting as amanuensis, found the strain of the relationship too much for her and retired to her brother's farm in Wales. Coleridge, resentful that Wordsworth should apparently have encouraged his sister-in-law's withdrawal, resolved shortly afterward to terminate his working relationship with William and Dorothy Wordsworth and to settle in London again.

The period immediately following was the darkest of his life. His disappointment with Wordsworth was followed by anguish when a wounding remark of Wordsworth's was carelessly reported to him. For some time he remained in London, nursing his grievances and producing little. Opium retained its powerful hold on him, and the writings that survive from this period are redolent of unhappiness, with self-dramatization veering toward self-pity.

In spite of this, however, there also appear signs of a slow revival, principally because for the first time Coleridge knew what it was to be a fashionable figure. A course of lectures he delivered during the winter of 1811–12 attracted a large audience. For many years Coleridge had been fascinated by William Shakespeare's achievement, and his psychological interpretations of the chief characters were new and exciting to his contemporaries. During this period, Coleridge's play *Osorio,* written many years before, was produced at Drury Lane with the title *Remorse* in January 1813.

Late Life and Works

In the end, consolation came from an unexpected source. In dejection, unable to produce extended work or break the opium habit, he spent a long period with friends in Wiltshire, where he was introduced to Archbishop Robert Leighton's commentary on the First Letter of Peter. In the writings of this 17th-century divine, he found a combination of tenderness and sanctity that appealed deeply to him and seemed to offer an attitude to life that he himself could fall back on. The discovery marks an important shift of balance in his intellectual attitudes. Christianity, hitherto one point of reference for him, now became his "official" creed. By aligning himself with the Anglican church of the 17th century at its best, he hoped to find a firm point of reference that would both keep him in communication with orthodox Christians of his time (thus giving him the social approval he always needed, even if only from a small group of friends) and enable him to pursue his former intellectual explorations in the hope of reaching a Christian synthesis that might help to revitalize the English church both intellectually and emotionally.

One effect of the adoption of this basis for his intellectual and emotional life was a sense of liberation and an ability to produce large works again. He drew together a collection of his poems (published in 1817 as *Sibylline Leaves*) and wrote *Biographia Literaria* (1817), a rambling and discursive but highly stimulating and influential work in which he outlined the evolution of his thought and developed an extended critique of Wordsworth's poems.

For the general reader *Biographia Literaria* is a misleading volume, since it moves bewilderingly between autobiography, abstruse philosophical discussion, and literary criticism. It has, however, an internal coherence of its own. The book's individual components—first an entertaining account of Coleridge's early life, then an account of the ways in which he became dissatisfied with the associationist theories of David Hartley and other 18th-century philosophers, then a reasoned critique of Wordsworth's poems—are fascinating. Over the whole work hovers Coleridge's veneration for the power of imagination: once this key is grasped, the unity of the work becomes evident.

A new dramatic piece, *Zapolya,* was also published in 1817. In the same year, Coleridge became associated for a time with the new *Encyclopaedia Metropolitana,* for which he planned a novel system of organization, outlined in his *Prospectus.* These were more settled years for Coleridge. Since 1816 he had lived in the house of James Gillman, a surgeon at Highgate, north of London. His election as a fellow of the Royal Society of Literature in 1824 brought him an annuity of £105 and a sense of recognition. In 1830 he joined the controversy that had arisen around the issue of Catholic Emancipation by writing his last prose work, *On the Constitution of the Church and State.* The third edition of Coleridge's *Poetical Works* appeared in time for him to see it before his final illness and death in 1834.

Coleridge's achievement has been given more widely varying assessments than that of any other English literary artist, though there is broad agreement that his enormous potential was never fully realized in his works. His stature as a poet has never been in doubt. In "Kubla Khan" and *The Rime of the Ancient Mariner* he wrote two of the greatest poems in English literature and perfected a mode of sensuous lyricism that is often echoed by later poets. But he also has a reputation as one of the most important of all English literary critics, largely on the basis of his *Biographia Literaria.* In Coleridge's view, the essential element of literature was a union of emotion and thought that he described as imagination. He especially stressed poetry's capacity for integrating the universal and the particular, the objective and the subjective, the generic and the individual. The function of criticism for Coleridge was to discern these elements and to lift them into conscious awareness, rather than merely to prescribe or to describe rules or forms.

In all his roles, as poet, social critic, literary critic, theologian, and psychologist, Coleridge expressed a profound concern with elucidating an underlying creative principle that is fundamental to both human beings and the universe as a whole. To Coleridge, imagination is the archetype of this unifying force because it represents the means by which the twin human capacities for intuitive, non-rational understanding and for organizing and discriminating thought concerning the material world are reconciled. It was by means of this sort of reconciliation of opposites that Coleridge attempted, with considerable success, to combine a sense of the universal and ideal with an acute observation of the particular and sensory in his own poetry and in his criticism.

John Keats

Born in 1795, John Keats received relatively little formal education. His father, a livery-stable manager, died in 1804, and his mother remarried almost immediately. Throughout his life Keats had close emotional ties to his sister, Fanny, and his two brothers, George and Tom. After the breakup of their mother's second marriage, the Keats children lived with their widowed grandmother at Edmonton, Middlesex. John attended a school at Enfield, two miles away, that was run by John Clarke, whose son Charles Cowden Clarke did much to encourage Keats's literary aspirations. At school Keats was noted as a pugnacious lad and was decidedly "not literary," but in 1809 he began to read voraciously. After the death of the Keats children's mother in 1810, their grandmother put the children's affairs into the hands of a guardian, Richard Abbey. At Abbey's instigation John Keats was apprenticed to a surgeon at Edmonton in 1811. He broke off his apprenticeship in 1814 and went to live in London, where he worked as a dresser, or junior house surgeon, at Guy's and St. Thomas' hospitals. His literary interests had crystallized by this time, and after 1817 he devoted himself entirely to poetry. From then until his early death, the story of his life is largely the story of the poetry he wrote.

Early Works

Charles Cowden Clarke had introduced the young Keats to the poetry of Edmund Spenser and the Elizabethans, and these were his earliest models. His first mature poem is the sonnet *On First Looking Into Chapman's Homer* (1816), which was inspired by his excited reading of George Chapman's classic 17th-century translation of the *Iliad* and the *Odyssey*. Clarke also introduced Keats to the journalist and contemporary poet Leigh Hunt, and Keats made friends in Hunt's circle with the young poet John Hamilton Reynolds and with the painter Benjamin Haydon. Keats's first book, *Poems*, was published in March 1817 and was written largely under "Huntian" influence. This is evident in the relaxed and rambling sentiments evinced and in Keats's use of a loose form of the heroic couplet and light rhymes. The most interesting poem in this volume is *Sleep and Poetry*, the middle section of which contains a prophetic view of Keats's own poetical progress. He sees himself as, at present, plunged in the delighted contemplation of sensuous natural beauty but realizes that he must leave this for an understanding of "the agony and strife of human hearts." Otherwise the volume is remarkable only for some delicate natural observation and some obvious Spenserian influences.

In 1817 Keats left London briefly for a trip to the Isle of Wight and Canterbury and began work on *Endymion*, his first long poem. On his return to London he moved into lodgings in Hampstead with his brothers. *Endymion* appeared in 1818. This work is divided into four 1,000-line sections, and its verse is composed in loose rhymed couplets. The poem narrates a version of the Greek legend of the moon goddess Diana's (or Cynthia's) love for Endymion, a mortal shepherd, but Keats puts the emphasis on Endymion's love for Diana rather than on hers for him. Keats transformed the tale to express the widespread Romantic theme of the attempt to find in actuality an ideal love that has been glimpsed heretofore only in imaginative longings. This theme is realized through fantastic and discursive adventures and through sensuous and luxuriant description. In his wanderings in quest of Diana, Endymion is guilty of an apparent infidelity to his visionary moon goddess and falls in love with an earthly maiden to whom he is attracted by human sympathy. But in the end Diana and the earthly maiden turn out to be one and the same. The poem equates Endymion's original romantic ardour with a more universal quest for a self-destroying transcendence in which he might achieve a blissful personal unity with all creation. Keats, however, was dissatisfied with the poem as soon as it was finished.

Personal Crisis

In the summer of 1818 Keats went on a walking tour in the Lake District (of northern England) and Scotland with his friend Charles Brown, and his exposure and overexertions on that trip brought on the first symptoms of the tuberculosis of which he was to die. On his return to London a brutal criticism of his early poems appeared in *Blackwood's Magazine*, followed by a similar attack on *Endymion* in the *Quarterly Review*. Contrary to later assertions, Keats met these reviews with a calm assertion of his own talents, and he went on steadily writing poetry. But there were family troubles. Keats's brother Tom had been suffering from tuberculosis for some time, and in the autumn of 1818 the poet nursed him through his last illness. About the same time, he met Fanny Brawne, a near neighbour in Hampstead, with whom he soon fell hopelessly and tragically in love. The relation with Fanny had a decisive effect on Keats's development. She seems to have been an unexceptional young woman, of firm and generous character, and kindly disposed toward Keats. But he expected more, perhaps more than anyone could give, as is evident from his overwrought letters. Both his uncertain material situation and his failing health in any case made it impossible for their relationship to run a normal course. After Tom's death (George had already gone to America), Keats moved into Wentworth Place with Brown; and in April 1819 Brawne and her mother became his next-door neighbours. About October 1819 Keats became engaged to Fanny.

The Year 1819

Keats had written *Isabella*, an adaptation of the story of the *Pot of Basil* in Giovanni Boccaccio's *Decameron*, in 1817–18, soon after the completion of *Endymion*, and again he was dissatisfied with his work. It was during the year 1819 that all his greatest poetry was written—*Lamia*, *The Eve of St. Agnes*, the great odes (*On Indolence, On a Grecian Urn, To Psyche*, *To a Nightingale, On Melancholy,* and *To Autumn*), and the two versions of *Hyperion*. This poetry was composed under the strain of illness and his growing love for Brawne. It is an astonishing body of work, marked by careful and considered development, technical, emotional, and intellectual.

Isabella, which Keats himself called "a weak-sided poem," contains some of the emotional weaknesses of *Endymion*, but *The Eve of St. Agnes* may be considered the perfect culmination of Keats's earlier poetic style. Written in the first flush of his meeting with Brawne, it conveys an atmosphere of passion and excitement in its description of the elopement of a pair of youthful lovers. Written in Spenserian stanzas, the poem presents its theme with unrivaled delicacy but displays no marked intellectual advance over Keats's earlier efforts. *Lamia* is another narrative poem and is a deliberate attempt to reform some of the technical weaknesses of *Endymion*. Keats makes use in this poem of a far tighter and more disciplined couplet, a firmer tone, and more controlled description.

The odes are Keats's most distinctive poetic achievement. They are essentially lyrical meditations on some object or quality that prompts the poet to confront the conflicting impulses of his inner being and to reflect upon his own longings and their relations to the wider world around him. All the odes were composed between March and June 1819 except *To Autumn*, which is from September. The internal debates in the odes centre on the dichotomy of eternal, transcendent ideals and the transience and change of the physical world. This subject was forced upon Keats by the painful death of his brother and his own failing health, and the odes highlight his struggle for self-awareness and certainty through the liberating powers of his imagination.

In the *Ode to a Nightingale* a visionary happiness in communing with the nightingale and its song is contrasted with the dead weight of human grief and sickness, and the transience of youth and beauty—strongly brought home to Keats in recent months by his brother's death. The song of the nightingale is seen as a symbol of art that outlasts the individual's mortal life. This theme is taken up more distinctly in the *Ode on a Grecian Urn*. The figures of the lovers depicted on the Greek urn become for him the symbol of an enduring but unconsummated passion that subtly belies the poem's celebrated conclusion, "Beauty is truth, truth beauty,—that is all ye know on earth, and all ye need to know." The Ode on Melancholy recognizes that sadness is the inevitable concomitant of human passion and happiness; the transience of joy and desire is an inevitable aspect of the natural process. But the rich, slow movement of this and the other odes suggests an enjoyment of such intensity and depth that it makes the moment eternal. *The Ode to Autumn* is essentially the record of such an experience. Autumn is seen not as a time of decay but as a season of complete ripeness and fulfillment, a pause in time when everything has reached fruition, and the question of transience is hardly raised.

These poems, with their rich and exquisitely sensuous detail and their meditative depth, are among the greatest achievements of Romantic poetry. With them should be mentioned the ballad *La Belle Dame sans merci*, of about the same time, which reveals the obverse and destructive side of the idyllic love seen in *The Eve of St. Agnes*.

Keats's fragmentary poetic epic, *Hyperion*, exists in two versions, the second being a revision of the first with the addition of a long prologue in a new style, which makes it into a different poem. *Hyperion* was begun in the autumn

Keats, detail of an oil painting by Joseph Severn, 1821; in the National Portrait Gallery, London. Courtesy of the National Portrait Gallery, London

of 1818, and all that there is of the first version was finished by April 1819. In September Keats wrote to Reynolds that he had given up *Hyperion*, but he appears to have continued working on the revised edition, *The Fall of Hyperion*, during the autumn of 1819. The two versions of *Hyperion* cover the period of Keats's most intense experience, both poetical and personal. The poem is his last attempt, in the face of increasing illness and frustrated love, to come to terms with the conflict between absolute value and mortal decay that appears in other forms in his earlier poetry.

The epic's subject is the supersession of the earlier Greek gods, the Titans, by the later Olympian gods. Keats's desire to write something unlike the luxuriant wandering of *Endymion* is clear, and he thus consciously attempts to emulate the epic loftiness of John Milton's *Paradise Lost*. The poem opens with the Titans already fallen, like Milton's fallen angels, and *Hyperion*, the sun god, is their one hope of further resistance, like Milton's Satan. There are numerous Miltonisms of style, but these are subdued in the revised version, as Keats felt unhappy with them; and the basis of the writing is revealed after all as a more austere and disciplined version of Keats's own manner. There is not enough of the narrative to make its ultimate direction clear; but it seems that the poem's hero was to be the young Apollo, the god of poetry. So, as *Endymion* was an allegory of the fate of the lover of beauty in the world, *Hyperion* was perhaps to be an allegory of the poet as creator. Certainly this theme is taken up explicitly in the new prologue to the second version.

The second version of *Hyperion* is one of the most remarkable pieces of writing in Keats's work; the blank verse has a new energy and rapidity, and the vision is presented with a spare grandeur, rising to its height in the epiphany of the goddess Moneta, who reveals to the dreamer the function of the poet in the world. It is his duty to separate himself from the mere dreamer and to share in the sufferings of humankind. The theme is not new to Keats—it appears in his earliest poetry—but it is here realized far more intensely. Yet with the threat of approaching death upon him, Keats could not advance any further in the direction that he foresaw as the right one, and the poem remains a fragment.

Last Years

There is no more to record of Keats's poetic career. The poems *Isabella*, *Lamia*, *The Eve of St. Agnes*, and *Hyperion* and the odes were all published in the famous 1820 volume, the one that gives the true measure of his powers. It appeared in July, by which time Keats was evidently doomed. He had been increasingly ill throughout 1819, and by the beginning of 1820 the evidence of tuberculosis was clear. He realized that it was his death warrant, and from that time sustained work became impossible. His friends Brown, the Hunts, and Brawne and her mother nursed him assiduously through the year. Percy Bysshe Shelley, hearing of his condition, wrote offering him hospitality in Pisa; but Keats did not accept. When Keats was ordered south for the winter, Joseph Severn undertook to accompany him to Rome. They sailed in September 1820, and from Naples they went to Rome, where in early December Keats had a relapse. Faithfully tended by Severn to the last, he died in Rome in February 1821.

It is impossible to say how much has been lost by Keats's early death. His reputation grew steadily throughout the 19th century, though as late as the 1840s the Pre-Raphaelite painter William Holman could refer to him as "this little-known poet." His influence is found everywhere in the decorative Romantic verse of the Victorian Age, from the early work of Alfred Tennyson onward. His general emotional temper and the minute delicacy of his natural observation were greatly admired by the Pre-Raphaelites, who both echoed his poetry in their own and illustrated it in their paintings. Keats's 19th-century followers on the whole valued the more superficial aspects of his work; and it has been largely left for the 20th century to realize the full range of his technical and intellectual achievement. His short life was devoted to the perfection of a poetry marked by vivid imagery, great sensuous appeal, and an attempt to express a philosophy through classical legend.

Percy Bysshe Shelley

Born in 1792, Percy Bysshe Shelley was the heir to rich estates acquired by his grandfather, Bysshe (pronounced *bish*) Shelley. Timothy Shelley, the poet's father, was a weak, conventional man who was caught between an overbearing father and a rebellious son. The young Shelley was educated at Syon House Academy (1802–04) and then at Eton (1804–10), where he resisted physical and mental bullying by indulging in imaginative escapism and literary pranks. Between the spring of 1810 and that of 1811, he published two Gothic novels and two volumes of juvenile verse. In the fall of 1810 Shelley entered University College, Oxford, where he enlisted his fellow student Thomas Jefferson Hogg as a disciple. But in March 1811, University College expelled both Shelley and Hogg for refusing to admit Shelley's authorship of *The Necessity of Atheism*. Hogg submitted to his family, but Shelley refused to apologize to his.

Late in August 1811, Shelley eloped with Harriet Westbrook, the younger daughter of a London tavern owner. By marrying her, he betrayed the acquisitive plans of his grandfather and father, who tried to starve him into submission but only drove the strong-willed youth to rebel against the established order. Early in 1812, Shelley,

Harriet, and her older sister Eliza Westbrook went to Dublin, where Shelley circulated pamphlets advocating political rights for Roman Catholics, autonomy for Ireland, and freethinking ideals. The couple traveled to Lynmouth, Devon, where Shelley issued more political pamphlets, and then to North Wales, where they spent almost six months in 1812–13.

Percy Bysshe Shelley, oil painting by Amelia Curran, 1819; in the National Portrait Gallery, London. Courtesy of the National Portrait Gallery, London

Lack of money finally drove Shelley to moneylenders in London, where in 1813 he issued *Queen Mab,* his first major poem—a nine-canto mixture of blank verse and lyric measures that attacks the evils of the past and present (commerce, war, the eating of meat, the church, monarchy, and marriage) but ends with resplendent hopes for humanity when freed from these vices. In June 1813 Harriet Shelley gave birth to their daughter Ianthe, but a year later Shelley fell in love with Mary Wollstonecraft Godwin, daughter of William Godwin and his first wife, *née* Mary Wollstonecraft. Against Godwin's objections, Shelley and Mary Godwin eloped to France on July 27, 1814, taking with them Mary's stepsister Jane (later "Claire") Clairmont. Following travels through France, Switzerland, and Germany, they returned to London, where they were shunned by the Godwins and most other friends. Shelley dodged creditors until the birth of his son Charles (born to Harriet, November 30, 1814), his grandfather's death (January 1815), and provisions of Sir Bysshe's will forced Sir Timothy to pay Shelley's debts and grant him an annual income.

Settling near Windsor Great Park in 1815, Shelley read the classics with Hogg and another friend, Thomas Love Peacock. He also wrote *Alastor; or The Spirit of Solitude,* a blank-verse poem, published with shorter poems in 1816, that warns idealists (like Shelley himself) not to abandon "sweet human love" and social improvement for the vain pursuit of evanescent dreams. By mid-May 1816, Shelley, Mary, and Claire Clairmont hurried to Geneva to intercept Lord Byron, with whom Claire had begun an affair. During this memorable summer, Shelley composed the poems "Hymn to Intellectual Beauty" and "Mont Blanc," and Mary began her novel *Frankenstein*. Shelley's party returned to England in September, settling in Bath. Late in the year, Harriet Shelley drowned herself in London, and on December 30, 1816, Shelley and Mary were married with the Godwins' blessing. But a Chancery Court decision declared Shelley unfit to raise Ianthe and Charles (his children by Harriet), who were placed in foster care at his expense.

In March 1817 the Shelleys settled near Peacock at Marlow, where Shelley wrote his twelve-canto romance-epic *Laon and Cythna; or, The Revolution of the Golden City* and Mary Shelley finished *Frankenstein*. They compiled *History of a Six Weeks' Tour* jointly from the letters and journals of their trips to Switzerland, concluding with "Mont Blanc." In November, *Laon and Cythna* was suppressed by its printer and publisher, who feared that Shelley's idealized tale of a peaceful national revolution, bloodily suppressed by a league of king and priests, violated the laws against blasphemous libel. After revisions, it was reissued in 1818 as *The Revolt of Islam*.

Because Shelley's health suffered from the climate and his financial obligations outran his resources, the Shelleys and Claire Clairmont went to Italy, where Byron was residing. They reached Milan in April 1818 and proceeded to Pisa and Leghorn (Livorno). That summer, at Bagni di Lucca, Shelley translated Plato's *Symposium* and wrote his own essay "On Love." He also completed a modest poem entitled *Rosalind and Helen,* in which he imagines his destiny in the poet-reformer "Lionel," who—imprisoned for radical activity—dies young after his release.

Thus far, Shelley's literary career had been politically oriented. *Queen Mab,* the early poems first published in 1964 as *The Esdaile Notebook, Laon and Cythna,* and most of his prose works were devoted to reforming society; and even *Alastor, Rosalind and Helen,* and the personal lyrics voiced the concerns of an idealistic reformer who is disappointed or persecuted by an unreceptive society. But in Italy, far from the daily irritations of British politics, Shelley deepened his understanding of art and literature and, unable to reshape the world to conform to his vision, he concentrated on embodying his ideals within his poems. His aim became, as he wrote in "Ode to the West Wind," to make his words "Ashes and sparks" as from "an unextinguished hearth," thereby transforming subsequent generations and, through them, the world. Later, as he became estranged from Mary Shelley, he portrayed even love in terms of aspiration, rather than fulfillment: "The desire of the moth for the star,/ Of the night for the morrow,/ The devotion to something afar/ From the sphere of our sorrow."

In August 1818, Shelley and Byron again met in Venice; the Shelleys remained there or at Este through October 1818. During their stay, little Clara Shelley (b. 1817) became ill and died. In "Lines Written Among the Euganean Hills" (published with *Rosalind and Helen*), Shelley writes how visions arising from the beautiful landscape seen from a hill near Este had revived him from despair to hopes for the political regeneration of Italy, thus transforming the scene into "a green isle . . . / In the deep wide sea of Misery." He also began *Julian and Maddalo*—in which Byron ("Maddalo") and Shelley debate human nature and destiny—and drafted Act I of *Prometheus Unbound*. In November 1818 the Shelleys traveled through Rome to Naples, where they remained until the end of February 1819.

Settling next at Rome, Shelley continued *Prometheus Unbound* and outlined *The Cenci,* a tragedy on the Elizabethan model based on a case of incestuous rape and patricide in sixteenth-century Rome. He completed this drama during the summer of 1819 near Leghorn, where the Shelleys fled in June after their other child, William Shelley

(b. 1816), died from malaria. Shelley himself terms *The Cenci* "a sad reality," contrasting it with earlier "visions . . . of the beautiful and just." Memorable characters, classic five-act structure, powerful and evocative language, and moral ambiguities still make *The Cenci* theatrically effective. Even so, it is a less notable achievement than *Prometheus Unbound: A Lyrical Drama,* which Shelley completed at Florence in the autumn of 1819, near the birth of Percy Florence Shelley, Mary Shelley's only surviving child. Both plays appeared about 1820.

In *Prometheus* Shelley inverts the plot of a lost play by Aeschylus in a poetic masterpiece that combines supple blank verse with a variety of complex lyric measures. In Act I, Prometheus, tortured on Jupiter's orders for having given mankind the gift of moral freedom, recalls his earlier curse of Jupiter and forgives him ("I wish no living thing to suffer pain"). By eschewing revenge, Prometheus, who embodies the moral will, can be reunited with his beloved Asia, a spiritual ideal transcending humanity; her love prevents him from becoming another tyrant when Jupiter is overthrown by the mysterious power known as Demogorgon. Act II traces Asia's awakening and journey toward Prometheus, beginning with her descent into the depths of nature to confront and question Demogorgon. Act III depicts the overthrow of Jupiter and the union of Asia and Prometheus, who—leaving Jupiter's throne vacant—retreat to a cave from which they influence the world through ideals embodied in the creative arts. The end of the act describes the renovation of both human society and the natural world. Act IV opens with joyful lyrics by spirits who describe the benevolent transformation of the human consciousness that has occurred. Next, other spirits hymn the beatitude of humanity and nature in this new millennial age; and finally, Demogorgon returns to tell all creatures that, should the fragile state of grace be lost, they can restore their moral freedom through these "spells":

To suffer woes which Hope thinks infinite;
To forgive wrongs darker than Death or Night;
To defy Power which seems Omnipotent;
To love, and bear; to hope, till Hope creates
From its own wreck the thing it contemplates . . .

Prometheus Unbound, which was the keystone of Shelley's poetic achievement, was written after he had been chastened by "sad reality" but before he began to fear that he had failed to reach an audience. Published with it were some of the poet's finest and most hopeful shorter poems, including "Ode to Liberty," "Ode to the West Wind," "The Cloud," and "To a Sky-Lark."

While completing *Prometheus Unbound* and *The Cenci,* Shelley reacted to news of the Peterloo Massacre (August 1819) in England by writing *The Masque of Anarchy* and several radical songs that he hoped would rouse the British people to active but nonviolent political protest. Later in 1819 he sent to England *Peter Bell the Third,* which joins literary satire of William Wordsworth's *Peter Bell* to attacks on corruptions in British society, and he drafted *A Philosophical View of Reform,* his longest (though incomplete) prose work, urging moderate reform to prevent a bloody revolution that might lead to new tyranny. Too radical to be published during Shelley's lifetime, *The Masque of Anarchy* appeared after the reformist elections of 1832, *Peter Bell the Third* and the political ballads in 1839–40, and *A Philosophical View of Reform* not until 1920.

After moving to Pisa in 1820, Shelley was stung by hostile reviews into expressing his hopes more guardedly. His "Letter to Maria Gisborne" in heroic couplets and "The Witch of Atlas" in ottava rima (both 1820; published 1824) combine the mythopoeic mode of *Prometheus Unbound* with the urbane self-irony that had emerged in *Peter Bell the Third,* showing Shelley's awareness that his ideals might seem naive to others. Late that year, *Oedipus Tyrannus; or, Swellfoot the Tyrant,* his satirical drama on the trial for adultery of Caroline (estranged wife of King George IV), appeared anonymously but was quickly suppressed. In 1821, however, Shelley reasserted his uncompromising idealism. *Epipsychidion* (in couplets) mythologizes his infatuation with Teresa ("Emilia") Viviani, a convent-bound young admirer, into a Dantesque fable of how human desire can be fulfilled through art. His essay *A Defence of Poetry* (published 1840) eloquently declares that the poet creates humane values and imagines the forms that shape the social order: thus each mind recreates its own private universe, and "Poets are the unacknowledged legislators of the World." *Adonais,* a pastoral elegy in Spenserian stanzas, commemorates the death of John Keats by declaring that, while we "decay/ Like corpses in a charnel," the creative spirit of Adonais, despite his physical death, "has outsoared the shadow of our night":

The One remains, the many change
and pass;
Heaven's light forever shines, Earth's
shadows fly;
Life, like a dome of many-coloured glass,
Stains the white radiance of Eternity,
Until Death tramples it to fragments.

The verse drama *Hellas* (published 1822) celebrates the Greek revolution against Turkish rule and reiterates the political message of *Laon and Cythna*—that the struggle for human liberty can be neither totally defeated nor fully realized, since the ideal is greater than its earthly embodiments.

After Byron's arrival in Pisa late in 1821, Shelley, inhibited by his presence, completed only a series of urbane, yet longing lyrics—most addressed to Jane Williams—during the early months of 1822. He began the drama "Charles the First," but soon abandoned it. After the Shelleys and Edward and Jane Williams moved to Lerici, Shelley began "The Triumph of Life," a dark fragment on which he was at work until he sailed to Leghorn to welcome his friend Leigh Hunt, who had arrived to edit a periodical called *The Liberal*. Shelley and Edward Williams drowned on July 8, 1822, when their boat sank during the stormy return voyage to Lerici.

Mary Shelley faithfully collected her late husband's unpublished writings, and by 1840, aided by Hunt and others, she had disseminated his fame and most of his writings. The careful study of Shelley's publications and manuscripts has since elucidated his deep learning, clear thought, and subtle artistry. Shelley was a passionate idealist and consummate artist who, while developing rational themes within traditional poetic forms, stretched language to its limits in articulating both personal desire and social altruism.

Lord Byron

Born in 1788, the boy who would become George Gordon Byron, 6th Baron Byron, was the son of the handsome and profligate Captain John "Mad Jack" Byron and his second wife, Catherine Gordon, a Scots heiress. After her husband had squandered most of her fortune, Mrs. Byron took her infant son to Aberdeen, Scotland, where they lived in lodgings on a meagre income; the captain died in France in 1791. George Gordon Byron had been born with

He was a member of the House of Lords, but George Gordon Byron is remembered for his poetry (and his rakish behaviour) more than his short-lived political career. Hulton Archive/Getty Images

a clubfoot and early developed an extreme sensitivity to his lameness. In 1798, at age 10, he unexpectedly inherited the title and estates of his great-uncle William, the 5th Baron Byron. His mother proudly took him to England, where the boy fell in love with the ghostly halls and spacious ruins of Newstead Abbey, which had been presented to the Byrons by Henry VIII.

After living at Newstead for a while, Byron was sent to school in London, and in 1801 he went to Harrow, one of

England's most prestigious schools. In 1803 he fell in love with his distant cousin, Mary Chaworth, who was older and already engaged, and when she rejected him she became the symbol for Byron of idealized and unattainable love. He probably met Augusta Byron, his half sister from his father's first marriage, that same year.

Education and Career

In 1805 Byron entered Trinity College, Cambridge, where he piled up debts at an alarming rate and indulged in the conventional vices of undergraduates there. The signs of his incipient sexual ambivalence became more pronounced in what he later described as "a violent, though *pure*, love and passion" for a young chorister, John Edleston. Byron's strong attachment to boys, often idealized as in the case of Edleston, was accompanied by his likewise strong attachment to women throughout his life. In 1806 Byron had his early poems privately printed in a volume entitled *Fugitive Pieces*, and that same year he formed at Trinity what was to be a close, lifelong friendship with John Cam Hobhouse, who stirred his interest in liberal Whiggism.

Byron's first published volume of poetry, *Hours of Idleness*, appeared in 1807. A sarcastic critique of the book in *The Edinburgh Review* provoked his retaliation in 1809 with a couplet satire, *English Bards and Scotch Reviewers*, in which he attacked the contemporary literary scene. This work gained him his first recognition.

On reaching his majority in 1809, Byron took his seat in the House of Lords, and then embarked with Hobhouse on a grand tour. They sailed to Lisbon, crossed Spain, and proceeded by Gibraltar and Malta to Greece, where they ventured inland to Ioánnina and to Tepelene in Albania. In Greece Byron began *Childe Harolde's Pilgrimage*, which he continued in Athens. In March 1810 he sailed with

Hobhouse for Constantinople (now Istanbul, Turkey), visited the site of Troy, and swam the Hellespont (present-day Dardanelles) in imitation of Leander. Byron's sojourn in Greece made a lasting impression on him. The Greeks' free and open frankness contrasted strongly with English reserve and hypocrisy and served to broaden his views of men and manners. He delighted in the sunshine and the moral tolerance of the people.

Byron arrived back in London in July 1811, and his mother died before he could reach her at Newstead. In February 1812 he made his first speech in the House of Lords, a humanitarian plea opposing harsh Tory measures against riotous Nottingham weavers. At the beginning of March, the first two cantos of *Childe Harold's Pilgrimage* were published by John Murray, and Byron "woke to find himself famous." The poem describes the travels and reflections of a young man who, disillusioned with a life of pleasure and revelry, looks for distraction in foreign lands. Besides furnishing a travelogue of Byron's own wanderings through the Mediterranean, the first two cantos express the melancholy and disillusionment felt by a generation weary of the wars of the post-Revolutionary and Napoleonic eras. In the poem Byron reflects upon the vanity of ambition, the transitory nature of pleasure, and the futility of the search for perfection in the course of a "pilgrimage" through Portugal, Spain, Albania, and Greece.

In the wake of *Childe Harold*'s enormous popularity, Byron was lionized in Whig society. The handsome poet was swept into a liaison with the passionate and eccentric Lady Caroline Lamb, and the scandal of an elopement was barely prevented by his friend Hobhouse. She was succeeded as his lover by Lady Oxford, who encouraged Byron's radicalism.

A print of Childe Harold's Pilgrimage *by British artist John Miller Watt. The multi-canto poem was written over several years and reveals details of Byron's own travels and mindset.* Private Collection/© Look and Learn/ The Bridgeman Art Library

During the summer of 1813, Byron apparently entered into intimate relations with his half sister Augusta, now married to Colonel George Leigh. He then carried on a flirtation with Lady Frances Webster as a diversion from this dangerous liaison. The agitations of these two love affairs and the sense of mingled guilt and exultation they aroused in Byron are reflected in the series of gloomy and remorseful Oriental verse tales he wrote at this time: *The Giaour* (1813); *The Bride of Abydos* (1813); *The Corsair* (1814), which sold 10,000 copies on the day of publication; and *Lara* (1814).

Seeking to escape his love affairs in marriage, Byron proposed in September 1814 to Anne Isabella (Annabella) Milbanke. The marriage took place in January 1815, and Lady Byron gave birth to a daughter, Augusta Ada, in December 1815. From the start the marriage was doomed by the gulf between Byron and his unimaginative and humorless wife. In January 1816, Annabella left Byron to live with her parents, amid swirling rumours centring on his relations with Augusta Leigh and his bisexuality. The couple obtained a legal separation. Wounded by the general moral indignation directed at him, Byron went abroad in April 1816, never to return to England.

Byron sailed up the Rhine River into Switzerland and settled at Geneva, near Percy Bysshe Shelley and Mary Godwin, who had eloped, and Godwin's stepsister, Claire Clairmont, with whom Byron had begun an affair in England. In Geneva he wrote the third canto of *Childe Harold* (1816), which follows Harold from Belgium up the Rhine River to Switzerland. It memorably evokes the historical associations of each place Harold visits, giving pictures of the Battle of Waterloo (whose site Byron visited), of Napoleon and Jean-Jacques Rousseau, and of the Swiss mountains and lakes, in verse that expresses both the most aspiring and most melancholy moods. A visit to the Bernese Oberland provided the scenery for the Faustian poetic drama *Manfred* (1817), whose protagonist reflects Byron's own brooding sense of guilt and the wider frustrations of the Romantic spirit doomed by the reflection that man is "half dust, half deity, alike unfit to sink or soar."

At the end of the summer the Shelley party left for England, where Claire gave birth to Byron's illegitimate daughter Allegra in January 1817. In October Byron and Hobhouse departed for Italy. They stopped in Venice, where Byron enjoyed the relaxed customs and morals of the Italians and carried on a love affair with Marianna Segati, his landlord's wife. In May he joined Hobhouse in Rome, gathering impressions that he recorded in a fourth canto of *Childe Harold* (1818). He also wrote *Beppo*, a poem in ottava rima that satirically contrasts Italian with English manners in the story of a Venetian menage-à-trois. Back in Venice, Margarita Cogni, a baker's wife, replaced Segati as his mistress, and his descriptions of the vagaries of this "gentle tigress" are among the most entertaining passages in his letters describing life in Italy. The sale of Newstead Abbey in the autumn of 1818 for £94,500 cleared Byron of his debts, which had risen to £34,000, and left him with a generous income.

In the light, mock-heroic style of *Beppo* Byron found the form in which he would write his greatest poem, *Don Juan*, a satire in the form of a picaresque verse tale. The first two cantos of *Don Juan* were begun in 1818 and published in July 1819. Byron transformed the legendary libertine Don Juan into an unsophisticated, innocent young man who, though he delightedly succumbs to the beautiful women who pursue him, remains a rational norm against which to view the absurdities and irrationalities of the world. Upon being sent abroad by his mother from his native Sevilla (Seville), Juan survives a shipwreck en route and is cast up on a Greek island, whence he is sold into slavery in Constantinople. He escapes to the Russian army, participates gallantly in the Russians' siege of Ismail, and is sent to St. Petersburg, where he wins the favour of the empress Catherine the Great and is sent by her on a diplomatic mission to England. The poem's story, however, remains merely a peg on which Byron could hang a witty and satirical social commentary. His most consistent targets are, first, the hypocrisy and cant underlying various social and sexual conventions, and, second, the vain ambitions and pretenses of poets, lovers, generals, rulers, and humanity in general.

Don Juan remains unfinished. Byron completed 16 cantos and had begun the 17th before his own illness and death. In *Don Juan* he was able to free himself from the excessive melancholy of *Childe Harold* and reveal other sides of his character and personality—his satiric wit and his unique view of the comic rather than the tragic discrepancy between reality and appearance.

Shelley and other visitors in 1818 found Byron grown fat, with hair long and turning gray, looking older than his years, and sunk in sexual promiscuity. But a chance meeting with Countess Teresa Gamba Guiccioli, who was only 19 years old and married to a man nearly three times her age, reenergized Byron and changed the course of his life. Byron followed her to Ravenna, and she later accompanied him back to Venice. Byron returned to Ravenna in January 1820 as Teresa's *cavalier servente* (gentleman-in-waiting) and won the friendship of her father and brother, Counts Ruggero and Pietro Gamba, who initiated him into the secret society of the Carbonari and its revolutionary aims to free Italy from Austrian rule. In Ravenna Byron wrote *The Prophecy of Dante*; cantos III, IV, and V of *Don Juan*; the poetic dramas *Marino Faliero*, *Sardanapalus*, *The Two Foscari*, and *Cain* (all published in 1821); and a satire on the poet Robert Southey, *The Vision of Judgment*, which contains a devastating parody of that poet laureate's fulsome eulogy of King George III.

Byron arrived in Pisa in November 1821, having followed Teresa and the Counts Gamba there after the latter had been expelled from Ravenna for taking part in an abortive uprising. He left his daughter Allegra, who had been sent to him by her mother, to be educated in a convent near Ravenna, where she died the following April. In Pisa Byron again became associated with Shelley, and in early summer of 1822 Byron went to Leghorn (Livorno), where he rented a villa not far from the sea. There in July the poet and essayist Leigh Hunt arrived from England to help Shelley and Byron edit a radical journal, *The Liberal.* Byron returned to Pisa and housed Hunt and his family in his villa. Despite the drowning of Shelley on July 8, the periodical went forward, and its first number contained *The Vision of Judgment*. At the end of September Byron moved to Genoa, where Teresa's family had found asylum.

Byron's interest in the periodical gradually waned, but he continued to support Hunt and to give manuscripts to *The Liberal*. After a quarrel with his publisher, John Murray, Byron gave all his later work, including cantos VI to XVI of *Don Juan* (1823–24), to Leigh Hunt's brother John, publisher of *The Liberal*.

By this time Byron was in search of new adventure. In April 1823 he agreed to act as agent of the London Committee, which had been formed to aid the Greeks in their struggle for independence from the Turks. In July 1823 Byron left Genoa for Cephalonia. He sent £4,000 of his own money to prepare the Greek fleet for sea service and then sailed for Missolonghi on December 29 to join Prince Aléxandros Mavrokordátos, leader of the forces in western Greece.

Byron made efforts to unite the various Greek factions and took personal command of a brigade of Souliot soldiers, reputedly the bravest of the Greeks. But a serious illness in February 1824 weakened him, and in April he contracted the fever from which he died at Missolonghi on April 19. Deeply mourned, he became a symbol of disinterested patriotism and a Greek national hero. His body was brought back to England and, refused burial in Westminster Abbey, was placed in the family vault near Newstead. Ironically, 145 years after his death, a memorial to Byron was finally placed on the floor of the Abbey.

Legacy

Lord Byron's writings are more patently autobiographic than even those of his fellow self-revealing Romantics. Upon close examination, however, the paradox of his complex character can be resolved into understandable elements. Byron early became aware of reality's imperfections, but the skepticism and cynicism bred of his disillusionment coexisted with a lifelong propensity to seek ideal perfection in all of life's experiences. Consequently, he alternated between deep-seated melancholy and humorous mockery in his reaction to the disparity between real life and his unattainable ideals. The melancholy of *Childe Harold* and the satiric realism of *Don Juan* are thus two sides of the same coin: the former runs the gamut of the moods of Romantic despair in reaction to life's imperfections, while the latter exhibits the humorous irony attending the unmasking of the hypocritical facade of reality.

Byron was initially diverted from his satiric-realistic bent by the success of *Childe Harold*. He followed this up with the Oriental tales, which reflected the gloomy moods of self-analysis and disenchantment of his years of fame. In *Manfred* and the third and fourth cantos of *Childe Harold* he projected the brooding remorse and despair that followed the debacle of his ambitions and love affairs in England. But gradually the relaxed and freer life in Italy opened up again the satiric vein, and he found his forte in the mock-heroic style of Italian verse satire. The ottava rima form, which Byron used in *Beppo* and *Don Juan*, was easily adaptable to the digressive commentary, and its final couplet was ideally suited to the deflation of sentimental pretensions:

Alas! for Juan and Haidée! they were
So loving and so lovely—till then never,
Excepting our first parents, such a pair
Had run the risk of being damn'd for ever;
And Haidée, being devout as well as fair
Had, doubtless, heard about the Stygian river,
And hell and purgatory—but forgot
Just in the very crisis she should not.

Byron's plays are not as highly regarded as his poetry. He provided *Manfred*, *Cain*, and the historical dramas with characters whose exalted rhetoric is replete with Byronic philosophy and self-confession, but these plays are truly successful only insofar as their protagonists reflect aspects of Byron's own personality.

Byron was a superb letter writer, conversational, witty, and relaxed, and the 20th-century publication of many previously unknown letters has further enhanced his literary reputation. Whether dealing with love or poetry, he cuts through to the heart of the matter with admirable incisiveness, and his apt and amusing turns of phrase make even his business letters fascinating.

Byron showed only that facet of his many-sided nature that was most congenial to each of his friends. To Hobhouse he was the facetious companion, humorous, cynical, and realistic, while to Edleston, and to most women, he could be tender, melancholy, and idealistic. But this weakness was also Byron's strength. His chameleon-like character was engendered not by hypocrisy but by sympathy and adaptability, for the side he showed was a real if only partial revelation of his true self. And this mobility of character permitted him to savour and to record the mood and thought of the moment with a sensitivity denied to those tied to the conventions of consistency.

Other Poets of the Early Romantic Period

In his own lifetime, William Blake's poetry was scarcely known. Sir Walter Scott, by contrast, was thought of as a major poet for his vigorous and evocative verse narratives *The Lay of the Last Minstrel* (1805) and *Marmion* (1808). Other verse writers were also highly esteemed. *The Elegiac Sonnets* (1784) of Charlotte Smith and the *Fourteen Sonnets* (1789) of William Lisle Bowles were received with enthusiasm by Samuel Taylor Coleridge. Thomas Campbell has been chiefly remembered for his patriotic lyrics such as *Ye Mariners of England* and *The Battle of Hohenlinden* (1807) and for the critical preface to his *Specimens of the British Poets* (1819). Samuel Rogers was known for his brilliant table talk (published 1856, after his death, as *Recollections of the Table-Talk of Samuel Rogers*), as well as for his exquisite but exiguous poetry. Another admired poet of the day was Thomas Moore, whose *Irish Melodies* began to appear in 1808. His highly coloured narrative *Lalla Rookh: An Oriental Romance* (1817) and his satirical poetry were also immensely popular.

Charlotte Smith was not the only significant woman poet in this period. Helen Maria Williams's *Poems* (1786), Ann Batten Cristall's *Poetical Sketches* (1795), Mary Robinson's *Sappho and Phaon* (1796), and Mary Tighe's *Psyche* (1805) all contain notable work.

Robert Southey was closely associated with William Wordsworth and Coleridge and was looked upon as a prominent member, with them, of the "Lake school" of

Charlotte Smith wrote poetry, but she later turned to writing novels to support her 12 children after leaving her husband. Her work challenged British mores of the time and championed the cause of class equality. Hulton Archive/ Getty Images

poetry. His originality is best seen in his ballads and his nine "English Eclogues," three of which were first published in the 1799 volume of his *Poems* with a prologue explaining that these verse sketches of contemporary life bore "no resemblance to any poems in our language." His "Oriental" narrative poems *Thalaba the Destroyer* (1801) and *The Curse of Kehama* (1810) were successful in their own time, but his fame is based on his prose work—the *Life of Nelson* (1813), the *History of the Peninsular War* (1823–32), and his classic formulation of the children's tale *The Three Bears*.

Robert Southey became England's poet laureate in 1813. Although he was grouped together with other "Lake poets," Southey approached his work in an entirely distinct and unique manner. Hulton Archive/Getty Images

George Crabbe wrote poetry of another kind. His sensibility, his values, much of his diction, and his heroic couplet verse form belong to the 18th century. He differs from the earlier Augustans, however, in his subject matter, concentrating on realistic, unsentimental accounts of the life of the poor and the middle classes. He shows considerable narrative gifts in his collections of verse tales (in which he anticipates many short-story techniques) and

Table Talk

The term *table talk* refers to informal conversation at, or as if at, a dining table. It applies especially to the social talk of a celebrity recorded for publication. Collections of such conversations exist from as early as the 3rd century CE, and the term has been in use in English since about the 16th century. The practice of recording conversations and sayings of the famous became especially popular in the 17th century. This material is especially useful for biographers and can be a form of literary biography in itself. One of the best-known examples of this is James Boswell's biography of Samuel Johnson, which consists mostly of Johnson's own words reproduced by Boswell.

great powers of description. His antipastoral *The Village* appeared in 1783. After a long silence, he returned to poetry with *The Parish Register* (1807), *The Borough* (1810), *Tales in Verse* (1812), and *Tales of the Hall* (1819), which gained him great popularity in the early 19th century.

Other Poets of the Later Period

John Clare, a Northamptonshire man of humble background, achieved early success with *Poems Descriptive of Rural Life and Scenery* (1820), *The Village Minstrel* (1821), and *The Shepherd's Calendar* (1827). Both his reputation and his mental health collapsed in the late 1830s. Clare spent the later years of his life in an asylum in Northampton; the poetry he wrote there was rediscovered in the 20th century. His natural simplicity and lucidity of diction, his intent observation, his almost Classical poise, and the unassuming dignity of his attitude to life make him one of the most quietly moving of English poets.

Thomas Lovell Beddoes, whose violent imagery and obsession with death and the macabre recall the Jacobean dramatists, represents an imagination at the opposite pole; metrical virtuosity is displayed in the songs and lyrical passages from his over-sensational tragedy *Death's Jest-Book* (begun 1825; published posthumously, 1850). Another minor writer who found inspiration in the 17th century was George Darley, some of whose songs from *Nepenthe* (1835) keep their place in anthologies. The comic writer Thomas Hood also wrote poems of social protest, such as *The Song of the Shirt* (1843) and *The Bridge of Sighs*, as well as the graceful *Plea of the Midsummer Fairies* (1827). Felicia Hemans's best-remembered poem, *Casabianca*, appeared in her volume *The Forest Sanctuary* (1825). This was followed in 1828 by the more substantial *Records of Woman*.

THE NOVEL

The death of Tobias Smollett in 1771 brought an end to the first great period of novel writing in English. Not until the appearance of Jane Austen's *Sense and Sensibility* in 1811 and Sir Walter Scott's *Waverley* in 1814 would there again be works of prose fiction that ranked with the masterpieces of Richardson, Fielding, Sterne, and Smollett.

It is possible to suggest practical reasons for this 40-year partial eclipse. The war with France made paper expensive, causing publishers in the 1790s and early 1800s to prefer short, dense forms, such as poetry. It might also be argued, in more broadly cultural terms, that the comic and realistic qualities of the novel were at odds with the new sensibility of Romanticism. But the problem was always one of quality rather than quantity. Flourishing as a form of entertainment, the novel nevertheless underwent several important developments in this period. One was the invention of the Gothic novel. Another was the appearance of a politically engaged fiction in the years immediately before the French Revolution. A third was the rise of women writers to the prominence that they have held ever since in prose fiction.

The sentimental tradition of Richardson and Sterne persisted until the 1790s with Henry Brooke's *The Fool of Quality* (1765–70), Henry Mackenzie's *The Man of Feeling* (1771), and Charles Lamb's *A Tale of Rosamund Gray and Old Blind Margaret* (1798). Novels of this kind were, however, increasingly mocked in the later years of the 18th century.

The comic realism of Fielding and Smollett continued in a more sporadic way. John Moore gave a cosmopolitan flavour to the worldly wisdom of his predecessors in *Zeluco* (1786) and *Mordaunt* (1800). Fanny Burney was a bridge between the 18th-century and Romantic-era traditions, fitting precisely into neither; she carried the comic realist manner into the field of female experience with the novels *Evelina* (1778), *Cecilia* (1782), and *Camilla* (1796). Her discovery of the comic and didactic potential of a plot charting a woman's progress from the nursery to the altar would be particularly important for several generations of female novelists.

Thomas Love Peacock is another witty novelist who combined an intimate knowledge of Romantic ideas with a satirical attitude toward them, though in comic debates rather than conventional narratives. *Headlong Hall* (1816), *Melincourt* (1817), and *Nightmare Abbey* (1818) are sharp accounts of contemporary intellectual and cultural fashions, as are the two much later fictions in which Peacock reused this successful formula, *Crotchet Castle* (1831) and *Gryll Grange* (1860–61).

Sir Walter Scott is the English writer who can in the fullest sense be called a Romantic novelist. After a successful career as a poet, Scott switched to prose fiction in 1814 with the first of the "Waverley novels." In the first phase of his work as a novelist, Scott wrote about the Scotland of the 17th and 18th centuries, charting its gradual transition from the feudal era into the modern world in a series of vivid human dramas. *Waverley* (1814), *Rob Roy* (1817), and *The Heart of Midlothian* (1818) are among the masterpieces of this period. In a second phase, beginning with *Ivanhoe* in 1819, Scott turned to stories set in medieval England. Finally, with *Quentin Durward* in 1823, he added European settings to his historical repertoire. Scott combines a capacity for comic social observation with a Romantic sense of landscape and an epic grandeur, enlarging the scope of the novel in ways that equip it to become the dominant literary form of the later 19th century.

Gothic Novel

The Gothic novel—a European Romantic, pseudomedieval fiction having a prevailing atmosphere of mystery and terror—had its heyday in the 1790s, but it underwent frequent revivals in subsequent centuries.

Called Gothic because its imaginative impulse was drawn from medieval buildings and ruins, such novels commonly used such settings as castles or monasteries equipped with subterranean passages, dark battlements, hidden panels, and trapdoors.

Horace Walpole can be credited with the genre's invention in *The Castle of Otranto* (1764). Walpole's intention was to "blend" the fantastic plot of "ancient romance" with the realistic characterization of "modern" (or novel) romance. Characters would respond with terror to extraordinary events, and readers would vicariously participate. Walpole's innovation was not significantly imitated until the 1790s, when—perhaps because the violence of the French Revolution created a taste for a correspondingly extreme mode of fiction—a torrent of such works appeared.

The most important writer of these stories was Ann Radcliffe, who distinguished between "terror" and "horror." Terror "expands the soul" by its use of "uncertainty and obscurity." Horror, on the other hand, is actual and specific. Radcliffe's own novels, especially *The Mysteries of Udolpho* (1794) and *The Italian* (1797), were examples of the fiction of terror. Vulnerable heroines, trapped in ruined castles, are terrified by supernatural perils that prove to be illusions.

Matthew Lewis, by contrast, wrote the fiction of horror. In *The Monk* (1796) the hero commits both murder and incest, and the repugnant details include a woman's imprisonment in a vault full of rotting human corpses. Some later examples of Gothic fiction have more-sophisticated agendas. Mary Wollstonecraft Shelley's *Frankenstein; or, The Modern Prometheus* (1818) is a novel of ideas that anticipates science fiction. James Hogg's *The Private Memoirs and Confessions of a Justified Sinner* (1824) is a subtle study of religious mania and split personality. Even in its more-vulgar examples, however, Gothic fiction can symbolically address serious political and psychological issues.

Easy targets for satire, the early Gothic romances died of their own extravagances of plot, but Gothic atmospheric machinery continued to haunt the fiction of such major 19th-century writers as the Brontë sisters, Edgar Allan Poe, Nathaniel Hawthorne, and even Dickens in *Bleak House* and *Great Expectations*.

Mary Wollstonecraft Shelley

(b. Aug. 30, 1797, London, Eng.—d. Feb. 1, 1851, London)

The English Romantic novelist Mary Wollstonecraft Shelley is best known as the author of *Frankenstein*.

The only daughter of William Godwin and Mary Wollstonecraft, she met the young poet Percy Bysshe Shelley in 1812 and eloped with him to France in July 1814. The couple were

Portrait of Mary Shelley, the author of Frankenstein; or, The Modern Prometheus. Hulton Archive/Getty Images

married in 1816, after Shelley's first wife had committed suicide. After her husband's death in 1822, she returned to England and devoted herself to publicizing Shelley's writings and to educating their only surviving child, Percy Florence Shelley. She published her late husband's *Posthumous Poems* (1824); she also edited his *Poetical Works* (1839), with long and invaluable notes, and his prose works. Her *Journal* is a rich source of Shelley biography, and her letters are an indispensable adjunct.

Mary Shelley's best-known book is *Frankenstein*; *or, The Modern Prometheus* (1818, revised 1831), a text that is part Gothic novel and part philosophical novel; it is also often considered an early example of science fiction. It narrates the dreadful consequences that arise after a scientist has artificially created a human being. (The man-made monster in this novel inspired a similar creature in numerous American horror films.) She wrote several other novels, including *Valperga* (1823), *The Fortunes of Perkin Warbeck* (1830), *Lodore* (1835), and *Falkner* (1837); *The Last Man* (1826), an account of the future destruction of the human race by a plague, is often ranked as her best work. Her travel book *History of a Six Weeks' Tour* (1817) recounts the continental tour she and Shelley took in 1814 following their elopement and then recounts their summer near Geneva in 1816.

Political Fiction

By the 1790s, realistic fiction had acquired a polemical role, reflecting the ideas of the French Revolution, though sacrificing much of its comic power in the process. One practitioner of this type of fiction, Robert Bage, is best remembered for *Hermsprong*; *or, Man as He Is Not* (1796), in which a "natural" hero rejects the conventions of contemporary society. The radical Thomas Holcroft published two novels, *Anna St. Ives* (1792) and *The Adventures of Hugh Trevor* (1794), influenced by the ideas of William Godwin. Godwin himself produced the best example of this political fiction in *Things as They Are; or, The Adventures of Caleb*

Williams (1794), borrowing techniques from the Gothic novel to enliven a narrative of social oppression.

Women and Prose Fiction

Women novelists contributed extensively to this ideological debate. Radicals such as Mary Wollstonecraft (*Mary*, 1788; *Maria*; *or, The Wrongs of Woman*, 1798), Elizabeth

Family portrait of Jane Austen. Her novels, which focus on common people, are credited with popularizing the novel as a modern literary form. Hulton Archive/Getty Images

Inchbald (*Nature and Art*, 1796), and Mary Hays (*Memoirs of Emma Courtney*, 1796) celebrated the rights of the individual. Anti-Jacobin novelists such as Jane West (*A Gossip's Story*, 1796; *A Tale of the Times*, 1799), Amelia Opie (*Adeline Mowbray*, 1804), and Mary Brunton (*Self-Control*, 1811) stressed the dangers of social change. Some writers were more bipartisan, notably Elizabeth Hamilton (*Memoirs of Modern Philosophers*, 1800) and Maria Edgeworth, whose long, varied, and distinguished career extended from *Letters for Literary Ladies* (1795) to *Helen* (1834). Her pioneering regional novel *Castle Rackrent* (1800), an affectionately comic portrait of life in 18th-century Ireland, influenced the subsequent work of Scott.

Jane Austen stands on the conservative side of this battle of ideas, though in novels that incorporate their anti-Jacobin and anti-Romantic views so subtly into love stories that many readers are unaware of them. Three of her novels—*Sense and Sensibility* (first published in 1811; originally titled "Elinor and Marianne"), *Pride and Prejudice* (1813; originally "First Impressions"), and *Northanger Abbey* (published posthumously in 1817)—were drafted in the late 1790s. Three more novels—*Mansfield Park* (1814), *Emma* (1815), and *Persuasion* (1817, together with *Northanger Abbey*)—were written between 1811 and 1817. Austen uses, essentially, two standard plots. In one of these a right-minded but neglected heroine is gradually acknowledged to be correct by characters who have previously looked down on her (such as Fanny Price in *Mansfield Park* and Anne Elliot in *Persuasion*). In the other an attractive but self-deceived heroine (such as Emma Woodhouse in *Emma* or Elizabeth Bennet in *Pride and Prejudice*) belatedly recovers from her condition of error and is rewarded with the partner she had previously despised or overlooked. On this slight framework, Austen constructs a powerful case for the superiority of the Augustan virtues of common sense, empiricism, and rationality so valued during the 18th century to the new "Romantic" values of imagination, egotism, and subjectivity. With Austen the comic brilliance and exquisite narrative construction of Fielding return to the English novel, in conjunction with a distinctive and deadly irony.

Although the birth of the English novel is to be seen in the first half of the 18th century, it is with Austen that the novel takes on its distinctively modern character in the realistic treatment of unremarkable people in the unremarkable situations of everyday life. In her six novels she created the comedy of manners of middle-class life in the England of her time, revealing the possibilities of "domestic" literature. Her repeated fable of a young woman's voyage to self-discovery on the passage through love to marriage focuses upon easily recognizable aspects of life. It is this concentration upon character and personality and upon the tensions between her heroines and their society that relates her novels more closely to the modern world than to the traditions of the 18th century. It is this modernity, together with the wit, realism, and timelessness of her prose style; her shrewd, amused sympathy; and the satisfaction to be found in stories so skillfully told, in novels so beautifully constructed, that helps to explain her continuing appeal for readers of all kinds. Modern critics remain fascinated by the commanding structure and organization of the novels, by the triumphs of technique that enable the writer to lay bare the tragicomedy of existence in stories of which the events and settings are apparently so ordinary and so circumscribed.

Sir Walter Scott

The Scottish novelist, poet, historian, and biographer Sir Walter Scott stands alone among Romantic novelists as both the inventor and the greatest practitioner of the historical novel.

Scott's father was a lawyer and his mother was the daughter of a physician. From his earliest years, Scott, who was born in 1771, was fond of listening to his elderly relatives' accounts and stories of the Scottish Border, and he soon became a voracious reader of poetry, history, drama, and fairy tales and romances. He had a remarkably retentive memory and astonished visitors by his eager reciting of poetry. His explorations of the neighbouring

Sir Walter Scott, 1870. © Photos.com/Jupiterimages

countryside developed in him both a love of natural beauty and a deep appreciation of the historic struggles of his Scottish forebears.

Scott was educated at the high school at Edinburgh and also for a time at the grammar school at Kelso. In 1786 he was apprenticed to his father as writer to the signet, a Scots equivalent of the English solicitor (attorney). His study and practice of law were somewhat desultory, for his immense youthful energy was diverted into social activities and into miscellaneous readings in Italian, Spanish, French, German, and Latin. After a very deeply felt early disappointment in love, he married, in December 1797, Charlotte Carpenter, of a French royalist family, with whom he lived happily until her death in 1826.

In the mid-1790s Scott became interested in German Romanticism, Gothic novels, and Scottish border ballads. His first published work, *The Chase, and William and Helen* (1796), was a translation of two ballads by the German Romantic balladeer G.A. Bürger. A poor translation of Goethe's *Götz von Berlichingen* followed in 1799. Scott's interest in border ballads finally bore fruit in his collection of them entitled *Minstrelsy of the Scottish Border*, 3 vol. (1802–03). His attempts to "restore" the orally corrupted versions back to their original compositions sometimes resulted in powerful poems that show a sophisticated Romantic flavour.

The work made Scott's name known to a wide public, and he followed up his first success with a full-length narrative poem, *The Lay of the Last Minstrel* (1805), which ran into many editions. The poem's clear and vigorous storytelling, Scottish regionalist elements, honest pathos, and vivid evocations of landscape were repeated in further poetic romances, including *Marmion* (1808), *The Lady of the Lake* (1810), which was the most successful of these pieces, *Rokeby* (1813), and *The Lord of the Isles* (1815).

Scott led a highly active literary and social life during these years. In 1808 his 18-volume edition of the works of John Dryden appeared, followed by his 19-volume edition of Jonathan Swift (1814) and other works. But his finances now took the first of several disastrous turns that were to partly determine the course of his future career. His appointment as sheriff deputy of the county of Selkirk in 1799 (a position he was to keep all his life) was a welcome supplement to his income, as was his appointment in 1806 as clerk to the Court of Session in Edinburgh. But he had also become a partner in a printing (and later publishing) firm owned by James Ballantyne and his irresponsible brother John. By 1813 this firm was hovering on the brink of financial disaster, and although Scott saved the company from bankruptcy, from that time onward everything he wrote was done partly in order to make money and pay off the lasting debts he had incurred. Another ruinous expenditure was the country house he was having built at Abbotsford, which he stocked with enormous quantities of antiquarian objects.

By 1813 Scott had begun to tire of narrative poetry, and the greater depth and verve of Byron's narrative poems threatened to oust him from his position as supreme purveyor of this kind of literary entertainment. In 1813 Scott rediscovered the unfinished manuscript of a novel he had started in 1805, and in the early summer of 1814 he wrote with extraordinary speed almost the whole of his novel, which he titled *Waverley*. It was one of the rare and happy cases in literary history when something original and powerful was immediately recognized and enjoyed by a large public. A story of the Jacobite rebellion of 1745, it reinterpreted and presented with living force the manners and loyalties of a vanished Scottish Highland society. The book was published anonymously, as were all of the many novels he wrote down to 1827.

In *Waverley* and succeeding novels Scott's particular literary gifts could be utilized to their fullest extent. First and foremost, he was a born storyteller who could place a large cast of vivid and varied characters in an exciting and turbulent historical setting. He was also a master of dialogue who felt equally at home with expressive Scottish regional speech and the polished courtesies of knights and aristocrats. His deep knowledge of Scottish history and society and his acute observation of its mores and attitudes enabled him to play the part of a social historian in insightful depictions of the whole range of Scottish society, from beggars and rustics to the middle classes and the professions and on up to the landowning nobility. The attention Scott gave to ordinary people was indeed a marked departure from previous historical novels' concentration on royalty. His flair for picturesque incidents enabled him to describe with equal vigour both eccentric Highland personalities and the fierce political and religious conflicts that agitated Scotland during the 17th and 18th centuries. Finally, Scott was the master of a rich, ornate, seemingly effortless literary style that blended energy with decorum, lyric beauty with clarity of description.

Scott followed up *Waverley* with a whole series of historical novels set in Scotland that are now known as the "Waverley" novels. *Guy Mannering* (1815) and *The Antiquary* (1816) completed a sort of trilogy covering the period from the 1740s to just after 1800. The first of four series of novels published under the title *Tales of My Landlord* was composed of *The Black Dwarf* and the masterpiece *Old Mortality* (1816). These were followed by the masterpieces *Rob Roy* (1817) and *The Heart of Midlothian* (1818), and then by *The Bride of Lammermoor* and *A Legend of Montrose* (both 1819). It was only after writing these novels of Scottish history that Scott, driven by the state of his finances and the need to satisfy the public appetite for historical fiction that he himself had created, turned to themes from English history and elsewhere. He thus wrote *Ivanhoe* (1819), a novel set in 12th-century England and one that remains his most popular book. *The Monastery* and *The Abbot* followed in 1820, and *The Pirate* and *The Fortunes of Nigel* appeared in 1822. Two more masterpieces were *Kenilworth* (1821), set in Elizabethan England, and the highly successful *Quentin Durward* (1823), set in 15th-century France. The best of his later novels are *Redgauntlet* (1824) and *The Talisman* (1825), the latter being set in Palestine during the Crusades.

In dealing with the recent past of his native country, Scott was able to find a fictional form in which to express the deep ambiguities of his own feeling for Scotland. On the one hand he welcomed Scotland's union with England and the commercial progress and modernization that it promised to bring, but on the other he bitterly regretted the loss of Scotland's independence and the steady decline of its national consciousness and traditions. Novel after novel in the "Waverley" series makes clear that the older, heroic tradition of the Scottish Jacobite clans (supporters of the exiled Stuart king James II and his descendants) had no place in the modern world; the true heroes of Scott's novels are thus not fighting knights-at-arms but the lawyers, farmers, merchants, and simple people who go about their business oblivious to the claims and emotional ties of a heroic past. Scott became a novelist by bringing his antiquarian and romantic feeling for Scotland's past into relation with his sense that Scotland's interests lay with a prudently commercial British future. He welcomed civilization, but he also longed for individual heroic action. It is this ambivalence that gives vigour, tension, and complexity of viewpoint to his best novels.

Scott's immense earnings in those years contributed to his financial downfall. Eager to own an estate and to act the part of a bountiful laird, he anticipated his income and involved himself in exceedingly complicated and ultimately disastrous financial agreements with his publisher, Archibald Constable, and his agents, the Ballantynes. He and they met almost every new expense with bills discounted on work still to be done; these bills were basically just written promises to pay at a future date. This form of payment was an accepted practice, but the great financial collapse of 1825 caused the four men's creditors to demand actual and immediate payment in cash. Constable was unable to meet his liabilities and went bankrupt, and he in turn dragged down the Ballantynes and Scott in his wake because their financial interests were inextricably intermingled. Scott assumed personal responsibility for both his and the Ballantynes' liabilities and thus courageously dedicated himself for the rest of his life to paying off debts amounting to about £120,000.

Everyone paid tribute to the selfless honesty with which he set himself to work to pay all his huge debts. Unfortunately, though, the corollary was reckless haste in the production of all his later books and compulsive work whose strain shortened his life. After the notable re-creation of the end of the Jacobite era in *Redgauntlet*, he produced nothing equal to his best early work, though his rapidity and ease of writing remained largely unimpaired, as did his popularity. Scott's creditors were not hard with him during this period, however, and he was generally revered as the grand old man of English letters. In 1827 Scott's authorship of the "Waverley" novels was finally made public. In 1831 his health deteriorated sharply, and he tried a continental tour with a long stay at Naples to aid recovery. He was taken home and died in 1832.

Scott gathered the disparate strands of contemporary novel-writing techniques into his own hands and harnessed them to his deep interest in Scottish history and his knowledge of antiquarian lore. The technique of the omniscient narrator and the use of regional speech, localized settings, sophisticated character delineation, and romantic themes treated in a realistic manner were all combined by him into virtually a new literary form, the historical novel. His influence on other European and American novelists was immediate and profound.

DISCURSIVE PROSE

The French Revolution prompted a fierce debate about social and political principles, a debate conducted in impassioned and often eloquent polemical prose. Richard Price's *Discourse on the Love of Our Country* (1789) was answered by Edmund Burke's conservative *Reflections on the Revolution in France* (1790) and by Wollstonecraft's *A Vindication of the Rights of Men* (1790) and *A Vindication of the Rights of Woman* (1792), the latter of which is an important early statement of feminist issues that gained greater recognition in the next century.

The Romantic emphasis on individualism is reflected in much of the prose of the period, particularly in criticism and the familiar essay. Among the most vigorous writing is that of William Hazlitt, a forthright and subjective critic whose most characteristic work is seen in his collections of lectures *On the English Poets* (1818), *On the English Comic Writers* (1819), and in *The Spirit of the Age* (1825), a series of valuable portraits of his contemporaries. *In The Essays of Elia* (1823) and *The Last Essays of Elia* (1833), Charles Lamb, an even more personal essayist, projects with apparent artlessness a carefully managed portrait of himself—charming, whimsical, witty, sentimental, and nostalgic. As his fine *Letters* show, however, he could on occasion produce mordant satire. Mary Russell Mitford's *Our Village* (1832) is another example of the charm and humour of the familiar essay in this period. Thomas De Quincey appealed to the new interest in writing about the self, producing a colourful account of his early experiences in *Confessions of an English Opium-Eater* (1821, revised and enlarged in 1856). His unusual gift of evoking states of dream and nightmare is best seen in essays such as *The English Mail Coach* and *On the Knocking at the Gate in Macbeth*; his essay *On Murder Considered as One of the Fine Arts* (1827; extended in 1839 and 1854) is an important anticipation of the Victorian Aesthetic movement. Walter Savage Landor's detached, lapidary style is seen at its best in some brief lyrics and in a series of erudite *Imaginary Conversations*, which began to appear in 1824.

The critical discourse of the era was dominated by the Whig quarterly *The Edinburgh Review* (begun 1802), edited by Francis Jeffrey, and its Tory rivals *The Quarterly Review* (begun 1809) and the monthly *Blackwood's Magazine* (begun 1817). Though their attacks on contemporary writers could be savagely partisan, they set a notable standard of fearless and independent journalism. Similar independence was shown by Leigh Hunt, whose outspoken journalism, particularly in his *Examiner* (begun 1808), was of wide influence, and by William Cobbett, whose *Rural Rides* (collected in 1830 from his *Political Register*) gives a telling picture, in forceful and clear prose, of the English countryside of his day.

Charles Lamb

Born in 1775, Charles Lamb went to school at Christ's Hospital, where he studied until 1789. He was a near contemporary there of Samuel Taylor Coleridge and of Leigh Hunt. In 1792 Lamb found employment as a clerk at East India House (the headquarters of the East India Company), remaining there until retirement in 1825. In 1796 Lamb's sister, Mary, in a fit of madness (which was to prove recurrent) killed their mother. Lamb reacted with courage and loyalty, taking on himself the burden of looking after Mary.

Lamb's first appearances in print were as a poet, with contributions to collections by Coleridge (1796) and by Charles Lloyd (1798). *A Tale of Rosamund Gray,* a prose romance, appeared in 1798, and in 1802 he published *John Woodvil,* a poetic tragedy. "The Old Familiar Faces" (1789) remains his best-known poem, although "On an Infant Dying As Soon As It Was Born" (1828) is his finest poetic achievement.

In 1807 Lamb and his sister published *Tales from Shakespear,* a retelling of the plays for children, and in 1809 they published *Mrs. Leicester's School,* a collection of stories supposedly told by pupils of a school in Hertfordshire. In 1808 Charles published a children's version of the *Odyssey,* called *The Adventures of Ulysses.*

In 1808 Lamb also published *Specimens of English Dramatic Poets Who Lived About the Time of Shakespear,* a selection of scenes from Elizabethan dramas; it had a considerable influence on the style of 19th-century English verse. Lamb also contributed critical papers on Shakespeare and on William Hogarth to Hunt's *Reflector.* Lamb's criticism often appears in the form of marginalia, reactions, and responses: brief comments, delicately phrased, but hardly ever argued through.

Lamb's greatest achievements were his remarkable letters and the essays that he wrote under the pseudonym Elia for *London Magazine,* which was founded in 1820. His style is highly personal and mannered, its function being to "create" and delineate the persona of Elia, and the writing, though sometimes simple, is never plain. The essays conjure up, with humour and sometimes with pathos, old acquaintances; they also recall scenes from childhood and from later life, and they indulge the author's sense of

Charles Lamb, c. *1810, in an engraving of a portrait by the writer William Hazlitt. A poet, critic, and novelist, Lamb is best known as an essayist and regular contributor to* London Magazine. Hulton Archive/Getty Images

playfulness and fancy. Beneath their whimsical surface, Lamb's essays are as much an expression of the Romantic movement as the verse of Coleridge and William Wordsworth. Elia's love of urban and suburban subject matter, however, points ahead, toward the work of the Victorian novelist Charles Dickens. The essay *On the Artificial Comedy of the Last Century* (1822) both helped to revive interest in Restoration comedy and anticipated the assumptions of the Aesthetic movement of the late

19th century. Lamb's first Elia essays were published separately in 1823; a second series appeared, as *The Last Essays of Elia,* in 1833.

William Hazlitt

Born in 1778, William Hazlitt spent his childhood in Ireland and North America, where his father, a Unitarian preacher, supported the American rebels. The family returned to England when William was nine, settling in Shropshire. At puberty the child became somewhat sullen and unapproachable, tendencies that persisted throughout his life. He read intensively, however, laying the foundation of his learning.

Having some difficulty in expressing himself either in conversation or in writing, he turned to painting and in 1802 traveled to Paris to work in the Louvre, though war between England and France compelled his return the following year. His friends, who already included Charles Lamb, William Wordsworth, and Samuel Taylor Coleridge, encouraged his ambitions as a painter; yet in 1805 he turned to metaphysics and the study of philosophy that had attracted him earlier, publishing his first book, *On the Principles of Human Action.* In 1808 he married Sarah Stoddart, and the couple went to live at Winterslow on Salisbury Plain, which was to become Hazlitt's favourite retreat for thinking and writing.

Although he successfully completed several literary projects, by the end of 1811 Hazlitt was penniless. He then gave a course of lectures in philosophy in London and began reporting for the *Morning Chronicle,* quickly establishing himself as critic, journalist, and essayist. His collected dramatic criticism appeared as *A View of the English Stage* in 1818. He also contributed to a number of journals, among them Leigh Hunt's *Examiner.* This association led to the publication of *The Round Table,* 2 vol. (1817), 52 essays of which 40 were by Hazlitt.

Also in 1817 Hazlitt published his *Characters of Shakespeare's Plays,* which met with immediate approval in most quarters. He had, however, become involved in a number of quarrels, often with his friends, resulting from the forcible expression of his views in the journals. At the same time, he made new friends and admirers (among them Percy Bysshe Shelley and John Keats) and consolidated his reputation as a lecturer, delivering courses *On the English Poets* (published 1818) and *On the English Comic Writers* (published 1819), as well as publishing a collection of political essays. His volume entitled *Lectures on the Dramatic Literature of the Age of Elizabeth* was prepared during 1819, but thereafter he devoted himself to essays for various journals, notably John Scott's *London Magazine*.

Hazlitt lived apart from his wife after the end of 1819, and they were divorced in 1822. He fell in love with the daughter of his London landlord, but the affair ended disastrously, and Hazlitt described his suffering in the strange *Liber Amoris; or, The New Pygmalion* (1823). Even so, many of his best essays were written during this difficult period and were collected in his two most famous books: *Table Talk* (1821) and *The Plain Speaker* (1826). Others were afterward edited by his son, William, as *Sketches and Essays* (1829), *Literary Remains* (1836), and *Winterslow* (1850) and by his biographer, P.P. Howe, as *New Writings* (1925–27). Hazlitt's other works during this period of prolific output included *Sketches of the Principal Picture Galleries in England* (1824), with its celebrated essay on the Dulwich gallery.

In April 1824 Hazlitt married a widow named Bridgwater. But the new wife was resented by his son, whom Hazlitt adored, and the couple separated after three years. Part of this second marriage was spent abroad, an experience recorded in *Notes of a Journey in France and Italy*

(1826). In France he began an ambitious but not very successful *Life of Napoleon,* 4 vol. (1828–30), and in 1825 he published some of his most effective writing in *The Spirit of the Age.* His last book, *Conversations of James Northcote*, was published in 1830, the year of his death. It recorded his long friendship with that eccentric painter.

Thomas De Quincey

As a child, Thomas De Quincey, who was born in 1785, was alienated from his solid, prosperous mercantile family by his sensitivity and precocity. At the age of 17 he ran away to Wales and then lived incognito in London (1802–03). There he formed a friendship with a young prostitute named Ann, who made a lasting impression on him. Reconciled to his family in 1803, he entered Worcester College, Oxford, where he conceived the ambition of becoming "the intellectual benefactor of mankind." He became widely read in many subjects and eventually would write essays on such subjects as history, biography, economics, psychology, and German metaphysics. While still at college in 1804, he took his first opium to relieve the pain of facial neuralgia. By 1813 he had become "a regular and confirmed opium-eater" (i.e., an opium addict), keeping a decanter of laudanum (tincture of opium) by his elbow and steadily increasing the dose; he remained an addict for the rest of his life.

De Quincey was an early admirer of *Lyrical Ballads*, and in 1807 he became a close associate of its authors, William Wordsworth and Samuel Taylor Coleridge. He rented Wordsworth's former home, Dove Cottage at Grasmere, on and off from 1809 to 1833. In 1817 De Quincey married Margaret Simpson, who had already borne him a son. Though he wrote voluminously, he published almost nothing. His financial position as head of a large family went from bad to worse until the appearance of *Confessions* (1821) in *London Magazine* made him famous. It was reprinted as a book in 1822.

The avowed purpose of the first version of the *Confessions* is to warn the reader of the dangers of opium, and it combines the interest of a journalistic exposé of a social evil, told from an insider's point of view, with a somewhat contradictory picture of the subjective pleasures of drug addiction. The book begins with an autobiographical account of the author's addiction, describes in detail the euphoric and highly symbolic reveries that he experienced under the drug's influence, and recounts the horrible nightmares that continued use of the drug eventually produced. The highly poetic and imaginative prose of the *Confessions of an English Opium-Eater* makes it one of the enduring stylistic masterpieces of English literature.

In 1856 he seized the opportunity provided by the publication of his collected works to rewrite the book that had made him famous. He added some descriptions of opium-inspired dreams that had appeared about 1845 in *Blackwood's Magazine* under the title *Suspiria de Profundis* ("Sighs from the Depths"). But by this time he had lost most of the accounts he had kept of his early opium visions, so he expanded the rather short original version of the *Confessions* in other ways, adding much autobiographical material on his childhood and his experiences as a youth in London. His literary style in the revised version of the *Confessions,* however, tends to be difficult, involved, and even verbose.

Among De Quincey's other autobiographical writings, the so-called *Lake Reminiscences* (first printed in *Tait's Magazine*, 1834–40), which deeply offended Wordsworth and the other Lake poets, remains of great interest, although it is highly subjective, not without malice, and unreliable in matters of detail. As a literary critic De Quincey is best known for his essay "On the Knocking at the Gate in *Macbeth*" (first printed in the *London Magazine,* October 1823), a brilliant piece of psychological insight and a classic of Shakespearean criticism.

De Quincey became increasingly solitary and eccentric, especially after his wife's death in 1837, and he often retreated for long periods into opium dreams. He died in 1859. Of the more than 14 volumes of his work, only the original *Confessions* is a definitive literary expression.

DRAMA

This was a great era of English theatre, notable for the acting of John Philip Kemble, Sarah Siddons, and, from 1814, the brilliant Edmund Kean. But it was not a great period of playwriting. The exclusive right to perform plays enjoyed by the "Royal" (or "legitimate") theatres created a damaging split between high and low art forms. The classic repertoire continued to be played but in buildings that had grown too large for subtle staging, and, when commissioning new texts, legitimate theatres were torn between a wish to preserve the blank-verse manner of the great tradition of English tragedy and a need to reflect the more-popular modes of performance developed by their illegitimate rivals.

This problem was less acute in comedy, where prose was the norm and Oliver Goldsmith and Richard Brinsley Sheridan had, in the 1770s, revived the tradition of "laughing comedy." But despite their attack on it, sentimental comedy remained the dominant mode, persisting in the work of Richard Cumberland (*The West Indian*, 1771), Hannah Cowley (*The Belle's Stratagem*, 1780), Elizabeth Inchbald (*I'll Tell You What*, 1785), John O'Keeffe (*Wild Oats*, 1791), Frederic Reynolds (*The Dramatist*, 1789),

George Colman the Younger (*John Bull*, 1803), and Thomas Morton (*Speed the Plough*, 1800). Sentimental drama received a fresh impetus in the 1790s from the work of the German dramatist August von Kotzebue; Inchbald translated his controversial *Das Kind Der Liebe* (1790) as *Lovers' Vows* in 1798.

Sentimental Comedy

Sentimental comedy is a dramatic genre primarily of the 18th century. The term denotes plays in which middle-class protagonists triumphantly overcome a series of moral trials. Such comedy aimed at producing tears rather than laughter. Sentimental comedies reflected contemporary philosophical conceptions of humans as inherently good but capable of being led astray through bad example. By an appeal to his noble sentiments, a man could be reformed and set back on the path of virtue. Although the plays contained characters whose natures seemed overly virtuous, and whose trials were too easily resolved, they were nonetheless accepted by audiences as truthful representations of the human predicament. Sentimental comedy had its roots in early 18th century tragedy, which had a vein of morality similar to that of sentimental comedy but had loftier characters and subject matter than sentimental comedy.

Writers of sentimental comedy included Colley Cibber and George Farquhar, with their respective plays *Love's Last Shift* (1696) and *The Constant Couple* (1699). The best-known sentimental comedy is Sir Richard Steele's *The Conscious Lovers* (1722), which deals with the trials and tribulations of its penniless heroine Indiana. The discovery that she is an heiress affords the necessary happy resolution. Steele, in describing the affect he wished the play to have, said he would like to arouse "a pleasure too exquisite for laughter." Sentimental comedies continued to coexist with such conventional comedies as Oliver Goldsmith's *She Stoops to Conquer* (1773) and Richard Brinsley Sheridan's *The Rivals* (1775) until the sentimental genre waned in the early 19th century.

By the 1780s, sentimental plays were beginning to anticipate what would become the most important dramatic form of the early 19th century—melodrama. Thomas Holcroft's *Seduction* (1787) and *The Road to Ruin* (1792) have something of the moral simplicity, tragicomic plot, and sensationalism of the "mélodrames" of Guilbert de Pixérécourt; Holcroft translated the latter's *Coelina* (1800) as *A Tale of Mystery* in 1802. Using background music to intensify the emotional effect, the form appealed chiefly, but not exclusively, to the working-class audiences of the "illegitimate" theatres. Many early examples, such as Matthew Lewis's *The Castle Spectre* (first performance 1797) and J.R. Planché's *The Vampire* (1820), were theatrical equivalents of the Gothic novel. But there were also criminal melodramas (Isaac Pocock, *The Miller and His Men*, 1813), patriotic melodramas (Douglas Jerrold, *Black-Eyed Susan*, 1829), domestic melodramas (John Howard Payne, *Clari*, 1823), and even industrial melodramas (John Walker, *The Factory Lad*, 1832). The energy and narrative force of the form would gradually help to revivify the "legitimate" serious drama, and its basic concerns would persist in the films and television of a later period.

Legitimate drama, performed at patent theatres, is best represented by the work of James Sheridan Knowles, who wrote stiffly neo-Elizabethan verse plays, both tragic and comic (*Virginius*, 1820; *The Hunchback*, 1832). The great lyric poets of the era all attempted to write tragedies of this kind, with little success. Coleridge's *Osorio* (1797) was produced (as *Remorse*) at Drury Lane in 1813, and Byron's *Marino Faliero* in 1821. Wordsworth's *The Borderers* (1797), Keats's *Otho the Great* (1819), and Percy Bysshe Shelley's *The Cenci* (1819) remained unperformed, though *The Cenci* has a sustained narrative tension that distinguishes it from the general Romantic tendency to subordinate action to character and produce "closet dramas" (for reading) rather

Portrait of James Sheridan Knowles, which first appeared in Fraser's Magazine *in 1833. As a dramatist, Knowles was particularly skilled at writing tragedies, such as* The Hunchback. Time & Life Pictures/Getty Images

than theatrical texts. The Victorian poet Robert Browning would spend much of his early career writing verse plays for the legitimate theatre (*Strafford*, 1837; *A Blot in the 'Scutcheon*, produced in 1843). But after the Theatre Regulation Act of 1843, which abolished the distinction between legitimate and illegitimate drama, demand for this kind of play rapidly disappeared.

Patent Theatres

The several London theatres that, through government licensing, held a monopoly on legitimate dramatic production there between 1660 and 1843 were called patent theatres. In reopening the theatres that had been closed by the Puritans, Charles II issued Letters Patent to Thomas Killigrew and William Davenant giving them exclusive right to form two acting companies. Killigrew established The King's Servants at Drury Lane, where they stayed. Davenant established The Duke of York's Servants at Lincoln's Inn Fields, from which they moved to Dorset Garden, finally settling at Covent Garden in 1732.

The legality of the patents, though continually questioned, was confirmed by Parliament with the Licensing Act of 1737, affirming Drury Lane and Covent Garden as the only legitimate theatres in England. Parliament began authorizing "theatre royals" outside of London in 1768, however, and in 1788 a bill was passed permitting local magistrates to license theatres outside a 20-mile radius of London. In London, evasion of the law was common, with unlicensed theatres offering undefined "public entertainments" and pantomime. In 1766 a third London theatre patent was issued to Samuel Foote for operation of the Haymarket Theatre during the summer months, and in 1807 the Earl of Dartmouth, as lord chamberlain, loosely interpreted the Licensing Act and began licensing other theatres in London. The Theatre Regulation Act of 1843 finally abolished the exclusive rights of the patent theatres to present legitimate drama.

EPILOGUE

To trace the history of English literature from the Restoration to the Romantic period is to move, historically, from one revolution to another. The first, the restoration of the monarchy that occurred when Charles II assumed the British throne in 1660, was not a violent, blood-in-the-streets revolution—indeed, the Restoration brought the chaos and disorder of the republican period to an end—but it represented a sweeping change in government and in political culture that upended all that had transpired in England during the preceding decade. The second, the French Revolution of 1789, had a profound effect on English Romantic writers, both directly—Wordsworth, for instance, who was sympathetic to the revolution, lived in France in the early 1790s and turned to the subject in his writing repeatedly—and indirectly.

The trajectory of English literature itself during this period was also one of revolutions, driven in large part by the ongoing expansion of the reading public. In the late 17th century, the size of a writer's audience in Britain was relatively small. By the early 19th century, however, the number of readers a writer might reach was vastly larger. The spread of literacy and the increasing mechanization of publishing were the most prominent causes. The remainder of the 19th century would witness the emergence of something approaching universal literacy in Great Britain—a revolution perhaps as important as the introduction of the printing press centuries earlier, since this audience had an insatiable appetite for reading material.

What did that audience demand? Many of the literary forms that, during the late 17th and early 18th centuries, were invented or otherwise reached the forms still known today: the novel, the newspaper, and the magazine, among others. These forms were themselves revolutions—in the sense, however, that they were adaptations of past forms made anew for a demanding, expanding audience.

And the writers themselves, some have argued, underwent a revolution in mind. While the 18th century was dominated by Neoclassicism—an aesthetic ideology of order, regularity, discipline—the Romantic era glorified the notion of the Byronic hero-writer, someone mad, bad, and dangerous to know, someone whose disorderly behaviour was valued as an expression of genius.

The period between the Restoration and the Romantic period was one marked by many changes. But through it all English literature was pushed onward by individual writers, from Bunyan to De Quincey, who did the everyday work of building on and breaking with the literary past.

GLOSSARY

allegory A symbolic fictional narrative that conveys a meaning not explicitly set forth in the narrative, such as a fable or parable.

amanuensis One who is employed to take dictation or to copy manuscript.

chapbook Small, inexpensive stitched tract that contains tales of popular heroes, legend, folklore, and other popular topics of the time.

discursive prose Writing that presents a formal and orderly, and usually extended, expression of thought on a particular subject; seen in the criticism and personal essays written during the Romantic period.

empiricism The view that all concepts originate in experience, that all concepts are about or applicable to things that can be experienced, or that all rationally acceptable beliefs or propositions are justifiable or knowable only through experience.

epistolary novel A novel told through the medium of letters written by one or more of the characters.

errata An error in printing or writing, especially such an error noted in a list of corrections and bound into a book.

heroic play Written in rhyming pentameter couplets, heroic plays presented characters of almost superhuman stature, and their predominant themes were exalted ideals of love, honour, and courage.

literati The literary intelligentsia.

mezzotint A method of engraving a metal plate by pricking its surface with innumerable small holes that hold ink and, when printed, produce large areas of tone.

moralistic Characterized by or expressive of a narrow moral attitude.

Neoclassical A revival in literature in the late 17th and 18th centuries, characterized by a regard for the classical ideals of reason, form, and restraint.

ottava rima Italian stanza form composed of eight 11-syllable lines, rhyming *abababcc*, used for heroic poetry in 17th- and 18th-century English verse.

pamphleteer One who engages in partisan arguments in writings, namely pamphlets.

pentameter In poetry, a line of verse containing five metrical feet; in iambic pentameter, each foot consists of an unstressed syllable followed by a stressed one.

perspicuous Clearly expressed or presented; easy to understand.

picaresque novel Usually a first-person narrative relating the adventures of a rogue or low-born adventurer as he drifts from place to place in an effort to survive.

Popish Plot The fictitious allegation that Jesuits were planning the assassination of King Charles II in order to bring his Roman Catholic brother, the Duke of York (afterward King James II), to the throne.

rodomontade Pretentious boasting or bragging; bluster.

sectarian Adhering or confined to the dogmatic limits of a sect or denomination; partisan.

tabula rasa A supposed condition that empiricists attribute to the human mind before ideas have been imprinted on it by the reaction of the senses to the external world of objects; the mind as a clean slate.

BIBLIOGRAPHY

THE RESTORATION AND THE 18TH CENTURY

Helpful introductions include Stephen Copley (ed.), *Literature and the Social Order in Eighteenth-Century England* (1984); Maximillian E. Novak, *Eighteenth-Century English Literature* (1983); and Pat Rogers (ed.), *The Eighteenth Century* (1978). The chapters on literature in John Brewer, *The Pleasures of the Imagination: English Culture in the Eighteenth Century* (1997), are another useful source.

A book that covers the whole period but focuses on a more-restricted topic is Jean H. Hagstrum, *Sex and Sensibility: Ideal and Erotic Love from Milton to Mozart* (1980). Among important thematic and general studies with a narrower chronological range are Marjorie Nicolson, *Science and Imagination* (1956, reprinted 1976); and David Nokes, *Raillery and Rage: A Study of Eighteenth-Century Satire* (1987).

Useful discussions of 18th-century novels are Michael McKeon, *The Origins of the English Novel* (1987, reissued 2002); John Mullan, *Sentiment and Sociability: The Language of Feeling in the Eighteenth Century* (1988); and John Richetti (ed.), *The Cambridge Companion to the Eighteenth-Century Novel* (1996).

Helpful for the poetry of the period are Ian Jack, *Augustan Satire: Intention and Idiom in English Poetry, 1660–1750* (1942, reissued 1978); Eric Rothstein, *Restoration and Eighteenth-Century Poetry, 1660–1780* (1981); and James Sutherland, *A Preface to Eighteenth-Century Poetry* (1948, reprinted 1970).

Richard Bevis, *The Laughing Tradition: Stage Comedy in Garrick's Day* (1980); and Robert D. Hume, *The Development of English Drama in the Late Seventeenth Century* (1978, reissued 1990), discuss aspects of theatre.

Literary criticism in the 18th century is surveyed in great detail in vol. 4 of H.B. Nisbet and Claude Rawson (eds.), *The Cambridge History of Literary Criticism, The Eighteenth Century* (1997).

THE ROMANTIC PERIOD

The general literary history of the period is presented in W.L. Renwick, *English Literature 1789–1815* (1963; also published as *The Rise of the Romantics*, 1990); and Ian Jack, *English Literature 1815–1832* (1963, reissued 1998), both part of the series *Oxford History of English Literature*. Marilyn Butler, *Romantics, Rebels, and Reactionaries: English Literature and Its Background, 1760–1830* (1981); and Jerome J. McGann, *The Romantic Ideology: A Critical Investigation* (1983), provide analytic surveys of the period. Works that focus on aspects of the literature include M.H. Abrams, *The Mirror and the Lamp: Romantic Theory and the Critical Tradition* (1953, reissued 1977), and *Natural Supernaturalism: Tradition and Revolution in Romantic Literature* (1971); Harold Bloom, *The Visionary Company: A Reading of English Romantic Poetry,* rev. and enlarged ed. (1971); Stuart Curran, *Poetic Form and British Romanticism* (1986); John O. Hayden (ed.), *Romantic Bards and British Reviewers* (1971); Gary Kelly, *English Fiction of the Romantic Period, 1789–1830* (1989); Karl Kroeber and Gene W. Ruoff (eds.), *Romantic Poetry: Recent Revisionary Criticism* (1993); Jerome J. McGann, *The Poetics of Sensibility* (1996); Theodore Redpath (compiler), *The Young Romantics and Critical Opinion, 1807–1824* (1973); and J.R. Watson, *English Poetry of the Romantic Period, 1789–1830*, 2nd ed. (1992).

HIGHLANDS
NORT
EDINBU
SEA
OR
GERMA
Peat
Bogs
IRISH
SEA
DUBLIN
OCE

INDEX

A

B

C

D

E

F

G

H

I

J

K

L

M

N

R

S

W

Y